the

TOP 20 MESSAGES FOR YOUTH MINISTRY

by

Jim Kochenburger

Foreword by

Jim Burns

Group

Loveland, Colorado

Dedication

I dedicate this book to my loving wife, Karen (the kindest, sweetest person I know), and my two unbelievably cool and fascinating children, Michael and Kristin. Thanks for being so understanding and supportive as I wrote this book. I love you, love you, love you!

Acknowledgements

The biggest thanks to my mentor in youth ministry, Jeanne Mayo. Your love, dedication, vision, wisdom, and unbelievable commitment—always giving first to your family then to the leaders and students in your youth ministry—inspires and awes me. Thanks for being a light to countless youth leaders across this land, teaching us that loving kids "like Jesus with skin on" is what real youth ministry is all about.

A big thanks to Dave Thornton and Joani Schultz for believing in this book (and the family devotions on the Web).

Thanks also to my editor, Amy Simpson, for her hard work, sensitive and caring edit, and ideas and advice that helped strengthen this book.

Another big thanks to Mom and Dad and the rest of my family for being so incredible to me my whole life. I love you all so much.

Thanks so much to Doug Miller for being such a great youth pastor, husband, and father and for sharing your activity ideas for the message "Pre' Sex—Don't Be Used, Abused, or Confused."

The Top 20 Messages for Youth Ministry

Copyright © 2001 Jim Kochenburger

All rights reserved. No part of this book may be reproduced in any manner whatsoever without prior written permission from the publisher, except where noted in the text and in the case of brief quotations embodied in critical articles and reviews. For information, write Permissions, Group Publishing, Inc., Dept. PD, P.O. Box 481, Loveland, CO 80539.

Visit our Web site: **www.grouppublishing.com**

Credits
Editor: Amy Simpson
Chief Creative Officer: Joani Schultz
Copy Editor: Deirdre Brouer
Art Director: Kari K. Monson
Cover Art Director and Designer: Jeff A. Storm
Computer Graphic Artist: Stephen Beer
Illustrator: Bryan Bandyk
Production Manager: Dodie Tipton

Unless otherwise noted, Scripture taken from the HOLY BIBLE, NEW INTERNATIONAL VERSION®. Copyright © 1973, 1978, 1984 by International Bible Society. Used by permission of Zondervan Publishing House. All rights reserved.

Library of Congress Cataloging-in-Publication Data
Kochenburger, James, 1962-
   The top 20 messages for youth ministry / by Jim Kochenburger ; foreword by Jim Burns.
     p. cm.
   ISBN 0-7644-2258-8 (alk. paper)
    1. Church group work with youth. 2. Christian education of young people. I. Title: Top twenty messages for youth ministry. II. Title.

BV4447 .K63 2001
268'.433--dc21

00-068954

10 9 8 7   10 09 08 07 06 05

Printed in the United States of America.

Contents

Foreword

by Jim Burns, Ph.D.

President, YouthBuilders (Formerly the National Institute of Youth Ministry)

One of the most freeing and finest pieces of advice I ever received as a youth worker was when an older, wiser youth pastor told me, "The essence of creativity is the ability to copy." I smiled. He said, "No, I really mean it." He went on to say, "I'm not talking about plagiarizing; I'm talking about using the great ideas of others and making them fit your youth group." Until that moment as a youth worker in a local church, I had been working too hard to produce mediocre youth messages on my own.

From that day on, I began looking to expert youth communicators to borrow their ideas and make them relevant for my youth group. In *The Top 20 Messages for Youth Ministry*, Jim Kochenburger has provided twenty (although you can squeeze more than twenty out of this book) practical, experiential messages that will make each biblical truth come alive to your students.

Here's why I am recommending this book to you:

I like Jim, and I believe in his ministry. He knows kids and youth workers. He has been in the trenches and now brings his expertise as a writer. When I am choosing to use other youth workers' messages from a book like this, I want to know if they are credible and live out their faith. Jim is and does!

The messages are biblical. There isn't a message in this book that doesn't bring home a biblical truth in a very meaningful way. Wasn't it the founder of Young Life, Jim Rayburn, who said, "It's a sin to bore a kid with the Bible"? Jim Kochenburger shows us that you can be both biblical and compelling.

Each message is experiential. Unfortunately, youth workers still talk too much and too long in youth group meetings. Edgar Dale, the famous educator from Ohio State years ago, taught that the most effective method of education is experiential learning. In fact, the average retention of a young person listening to a lecture is about 5 to 10 percent, but if students participate in experiential education, not only do they enjoy it much more, they also retain up to 85 percent of the message.

The messages have a variety of activities. I like books like this one because I can pick and choose from a number of options on each topic. If I don't think the skit will work for my group, I don't have to throw out the whole message. Odds are, the movie clip is a winner or vice versa. Your students have a variety of learning styles, and this message book hits all those styles.

If you don't feel very creative or you are running low on great ideas, take the advice of my friend, and don't be afraid to copy someone with great experiences. You can still come up with wonderful messages and have the time to build relationships with the kids in your group. Go ahead, continue developing an extraordinary resource library, and put this book very close to the top.

Introduction

My worst sermon was my first sermon. From that experience I learned that failure is not fatal—you can give an exceedingly poor sermon and still survive (no matter how much you might have prayed that God would strike you right there on the spot—or graze you with a bolt and knock you out so you could at least gain the "sympathy factor" from the audience). I didn't die, the sun rose the next day just as it had every day before, my calling remained intact, the congregation still loved me, and I lived to preach another day.

I remember that experience as if it were yesterday. There I was on youth day, a youth ministry volunteer speaking to a congregation of about seven hundred people, poor souls who no doubt will be rewarded in heaven for what they suffered on earth that day (forgive me, Life and Praise Temple in Auburndale, Florida). My topic that day was "Knowing God," and the text, I think, was Philippians 3 (but it's anybody's guess and kind of a blur now). While preparing for the message, I remember reading a quote from some famous minister or great preacher who said, "If you can get out of preaching—do it!" I wondered if it was God speaking. In retrospect, it probably was. (It was one of those moments when you wonder if your life is just serving as a warning for others.)

Now if you haven't inflicted your worst message yet on unsuspecting souls, be ready—you'll probably have your turn! But not if I can help it.

What you hold in your hands is bad-sermon repellent, bad-message insurance (not insuring you will give a bad message but guarding you against it!), or stinky-message deodorant.

This Book Offers You...

• twenty next-level message outlines to slice and dice and make your own,

• funny and dramatic skits,

• more than twenty great stories and illustrations,

• more than twenty great movie-clip ideas, and

• more than fifty great activity ideas to help you make your messages R.E.A.L. (relational, experiential, applicable, learner-based, and life-changing)!

So whether you're creatively challenged or a creative genius, wooden and stoic or an orator oozing with charisma and humor, a masterful speaker or a novice, this book is jampacked with cool ideas to enhance or add to your messages. Enjoy!

(Oh, and don't forget the extra family devotions and ideas that go with this book. We've added them to our Web site at www.youthministry.com/family_devos!)

How to Use This Book

Though I don't doubt your intelligence, you probably should read about how to use this book so you can get the most from it.

This book contains twenty outstanding messages, or "youth talk" outlines, and they're crying out to you—*begging* you—to tear them apart and make them your own. So slice and dice to your heart's content. It won't hurt my feelings.

Flip to one of the first messages. You'll notice that each message contains italics and regular text. The italics are instructions for you, the speaker, and the regular text suggests what to say to your students. Note the airy format, a layout that says to you, "This is easy, you can do this." And you can. Let's take a stroll through the format together. Ready?

Title—Sure, this is pretty self-explanatory. The titles separate one message from another and provide the gist of what the message is about. If you don't like it, create your own! Just toss it out there even a week in advance so those students of yours who hang on your every word (you know, the 99 percent in your youth ministry) can get really excited and will hardly be able to wait to hear what you have to say.

Topics—This heading tells you specifically what the message is about. The first topic listed is the primary theme, and the rest are related themes that are also addressed during the message.

Scripture Base—Each message is based on the verses and passages listed here. (They really tie in!) The message explores every passage listed.

The Point—Seasoned leaders know better than to try to dump fifty points and subpoints on students. The information just goes in one ear and disappears in brain gases. The Point for each message is your focus—the heart of the message. Everything you say or do in the message should revolve around this. Use it as the compass for your talk so you don't come across as unfocused, unclear, dazed, confused, and rambling down every rabbit trail your wonderfully creative mind can dream up!

Stuff You'll Need—OK, you'll always need a Bible and a chalkboard and chalk or newsprint and markers. That's a given. In this list you'll find the unique items you'll need for each message. Most of the items are easy to get, and those that aren't are well worth the effort because of the impact they'll have on students.

Preparation—Most of these outlines require a modest amount of preparation. A few require no preparation at all. But remember: The most important preparation is preparing your heart to deliver your active message with power and impact.

Introduction—This often features an activity to get the ball rolling. Students may do a pair-share (discuss questions with a partner) or participate in a quick, simple activity. Either of these tools provides a great way to get students involved immediately in your message.

The Message—This section contains all the Key Points of your message. You'll also find Activators and Leadership Tips as well as Keepin' It Real boxes. Let me explain each of these briefly.

- **Key Points**—These are the main points of your message outline. You can use these short, memorable statements as the guideposts for your message. They carry the flow of the message and keep things moving forward.

- **Activators**—These fun, multisensory activities can be found throughout the active message. Notice that connection? *Active* message…*Activator?* Now if you're a true-blue-preacher type, you'll be thinking right now, "I'm not a fun-and-games person. Besides, activities will distract students from my talk, and…" Hold on! Before you skip over these activities, consider these hard facts, based on years of research in education (see *The Dirt on Learning* by Thom and Joani Schultz):

  1. The more that students get *actively involved* in the message, the more of the message they'll remember and apply to their lives. Involving students allows the message to go deeper into their hearts and minds.

  2. Not all students learn the same way. Some are visual learners, some are auditory learners, and some are tactile learners. The more senses (sight, hearing, touch, taste, and

smell) you engage, the more effectively you will reach *all* of your students and help them learn.

3. The more lecture-based information we dump on students at one time—gobs of Bible verses, for example, and tons of points and subpoints—the less they'll actually comprehend and apply to their lives. *Less really is more!* Rather than acting as a distraction from your message, the Activators help you *reinforce* the Key Points you want students to learn—by involving students directly in the learning experience.

4. If you're still uncomfortable with the idea of using activities in your messages, take on this simple challenge: Just try it! Then watch how students respond. We're confident you'll quickly see the positive impact on your students. You may hear them talk about the activity and what they learned from it for weeks after the event. Give it a shot! It works!

• **Leadership Tips**—These informative tips help you adapt your message for groups of different sizes and provide helpful tips for making your message go smoothly.

• **Keepin' It Real!**—This box provides a timely story cue, asking you to share a personal story from your day-to-day life (or someone else's) that will help illustrate a point to students.

Throughout the messages, we've also included a whole bunch of great stories of our own that you can use to illustrate your points.

Closing Challenge—This section offers a summary of the message, then leads students right into the Commitment Cores. After any message, it's important for students to have the opportunity to act on what they've learned. In core groups of two or three, students will share with one another their struggles, questions, and what they've learned from your message. And they'll pray for one another according to what each person in their core groups has shared.

Reality Bite—This box suggests projects, ministry ideas, homework, or creative field trips to provide students with real-life opportunities to explore more deeply what they've learned.

Give the outlines in this book a careful evaluation. Then try them, and get responses from students to see how well they work. If you do, you'll discover that *The Top 20 Messages for Youth Ministry* really can help you be a more effective speaker and teacher and can help your students grow up in their Christian faith.

Remember to fill out the survey in the back of the book to let us know how this resource worked for you! If you like it, we'll make more!

Very Important Information

• **Legal Use of Video Clips**—According to federal copyright laws, rented or personal videos cannot be used for any purposes other than home viewing. In order to show a video clip in your youth ministry, it's best to obtain a license. For more information about copyright laws or to obtain a blanket license for a small fee, contact the Motion Picture Licensing Corporation at www.mplc.com or call 1-800-462-8855. (Also see page 10 for "More Important Video-Clip Information.")

• **Free Family Devotions on the Net!**—Group Publishing and the author of this book share a strong desire and calling to minister to the whole family. We've created family devotions for parents and teenagers, with topics directly related to the topics of the messages you'll find in this book.

As the original purchaser of this book, you have permission to download these devotions from our Web site at no cost. Then you can make them available to your students' parents. These devotions are full of fun, non-cheesy, creative ideas that parents can use at home to reinforce what you're teaching! We encourage you to pick these up at www.youthministry.com/family_devos.

• **Free Ideas on the Net!**—We have so many good ideas that we couldn't fit them all into this book, so we've put them on the Internet for you to pick up and use as you like. These include skits, activities, and video-clip illustrations. See www.youthministry.com/family_devos. You have permission to download these ideas for your personal use if you're the original purchaser of this book.

• **More Important Video-Clip Information**—In order to locate the video clips, start your VCR timer at 00:00:00 when the studio logo appears at the beginning of the film. All of the suggested start and stop times are rounded to the nearest fifteen-second interval. I've also suggested visual cues to clue you in on the action at the beginning and end of each video segment. Each clip is only one to five minutes long so that it will add to the message without distracting students from your main focus.

Be aware that if you use the video clip, students may interpret it as your endorsement of the whole film. Do some research before you show any movie. If you aren't sure whether to use one, tell some parents what clip you intend to use and the point you intend to make, and ask if they feel it's appropriate! Be prepared to voice a disclaimer to your students if necessary, emphasizing that you value the clip you've shown but explaining your concerns about other aspects of the movie.

And before you show the movie, *preview the clip!* Each of the specific clips I've recommended is free of questionable content, although the scenes before and after the clip may not always be up to par. So be sure to have the VCR cued to the right spot, and be especially careful if you have one of those VCRs that roll back a few seconds when stopped.

Don't Be a Fool, Keep Your Cool

Topics

Anger, violence, becoming a peacemaker

Scripture Base

Genesis 4:1-12, 16; Proverbs 29:11; Ephesians 4:26-27; James 1:19-20

The Point

We must control our anger, kill it with kindness, and seek peace with all people in all circumstances.

Stuff You'll Need

TV and VCR, *The Waterboy* movie (Touchstone Pictures), copies of the "Explosive Attitudes" handout (p. 16), forty-five feet of string, scissors

Preparation

Before the session, cut a five-foot length of string. Put this in your pocket. Put the rest of the string in your other pocket.

Write the Commitment Cores questions on a chalkboard or a sheet of newsprint.

Introduction

The Waterboy

To show an extreme, though humorous, look at anger, play a clip from The Waterboy. *Begin the video at 24 minutes, 15 seconds when the professor enters the class. End the clip when students pull Bobby off the professor at about 26 minutes, 15 seconds.*

For 160 more great video-clip ideas like this one, see Group's BlockBuster Movie Illustrations by Bryan Belknap.

Turn to someone beside you, and tell him or her the funniest or most embarrassing story of you expressing anger. Then discuss whether or not anger is always a choice.

Allow students two minutes to share, then have several volunteers tell the whole group some of what they heard or shared.

Although Bobby's anger is funny, what's going on in our society is often far from funny. Stories of road rage, air rage, crimes of passion, drive-by shootings, and people shooting others who look at them the wrong way are everywhere. People seem to be getting meaner; their fuses are shorter; they're better armed. It's getting pretty wild. Here's just one example.

Murder at the Hockey Rink

Read students the following true story.

Not long ago a man was murdered by another man at their sons' hockey practice. The two had an argument over rough play by the youngsters. The argument quickly escalated and one man, Thomas Junta, beat the other man, Michael Costin, to death as their sons and other children—and a number of adults—stood by and watched.

A man, a single father with children, was beaten to death in front of his kids over a foolish argument. The other man faces up to twenty years in prison for manslaughter. Two families lose their dads over an argument that got out of hand. If we can't control our anger, we may be just one or two bad decisions away from a rage that could end life as we know it. There is perhaps no better way to be salt in our society than to be a voice for peace.

This didn't have to happen. It proves once again that anger left unchallenged or handled improperly can have tragic consequences.

Read Proverbs 29:11.

Let's take a look at how to control our anger and seek peace and kindness.

The Message

Key Point #1: C=Choose to Cool off.

Read or summarize Genesis 4:1-12, 16.

Although it may seem as if Cain made only one bad choice (killing his brother), what he did was actually the result of a number of bad choices, and each one escalated rather than diffused his anger. If Cain had made even one choice differently, we might have had an entirely different outcome to this story. Our choices can make all the difference.

Let's do an activity to illustrate what choices mean.

Leadership Tip

As students react to this situation, note any differences between the reactions of the guys and girls in your group. Address this as you feel it's appropriate. Be prepared for a lot of emotion in the discussion of this realistic scenario.

Dave's Disrespect Deal

Read aloud the following account of a young man responding to some disrespect. Have group members stop you each time the main character, Dave, has a choice to make to either escalate his anger or diffuse it by seeking peace. Have the group say when Dave has a choice, name what the options are, and role-play Dave trying to make peace.

Dave is cruising with his girlfriend, Tonya, and two of his boys, Duke and Tommy. Dave has a cool car and is pretty proud of it. He's also proud of Tonya. She's beautiful. They've been dating for a while. Duke and Tommy are along for the ride.

Dave pulls into a parking place beside another car at the movie theater. He notices three guys in the car with music blaring. He feels one of the guys giving him a "you're a punk" look. Then he sees one of the guys checking Tonya out as she gets out of the car. Dave is starting to feel a little tense. He starts thinking of things to say; he's already thinking the guys in the other car are starting something.

As Tonya passes by, one of the guys whistles at her, another looks at her and says, "Mm-mm-mm," and the third says, "Hey, baby, want a ride?" Dave walks up to the car with Duke and Tommy close behind. "I think you punks owe the lady an apology." The guys in the car just laugh at Dave, and Dave gets hot—he can feel his face turning blood-red. "It's go time," Dave says, and he opens the driver's door.

The driver says, "Think about it. You and your boys are soft—we would mess you up. Why don't you little boys go and enjoy your cartoon? Of course, the lovely lady can stay with us. We'll treat her right."

Dave jumped at the driver while Duke rolled over the hood to get the guy on the other side. Tommy opened the other door and pulled the third guy out.

Dave ended up in the hospital with several broken bones after the driver took it to him with a baseball bat he pulled from under his seat.

• What's your reaction to this situation and our discussion? Why?

• This situation was really a tough one. What are some other situations in which it can be tough to choose peace over anger? Why?

• Do you believe God can help you pursue peace rather than anger in any and all situations, no matter what? Explain.

• What are some things we can think of or do to help us pursue peace in situations like this?

Read Ephesians 4:26-27 and James 1:19-20.

Though it almost never feels like it, the truth is you always have a choice to diffuse and control your temper or escalate your anger and lose it.

You also need to know that the right choice isn't always the coolest choice. When you choose to be kind or a peacemaker, some people are only going to see you as soft and weak. To Jesus that's a risk worth taking, and it's in the best long-term interest for everyone involved. You may feel like a sucker or a chump at the moment, but you'll earn respect and blessing over the long haul for your commitment to peace.

Any weakling can fly into a rage over the slightest thing. It takes a strong person to keep the peace. Choose to be a peacemaker.

Key Point #2: O=Own your anger.

Read Genesis 4:9-11.

Cain tried to hide the fruit of his anger, the killing of his brother. He even tried to hide it from God. He didn't want to own up to it. Your anger is you; it's yours; it's a part of you whether you like it or not.

Each of us has said to others, "You make me so angry!" But the truth is no one can make us become angry. It's our choice, and it's our anger. Blaming others and trying to justify our angry attitudes and actions only entrenches them deeper in our hearts.

Own your anger. It belongs to you. It's your responsibility to control. If you never own it, you'll never empower yourself to dethrone its influence in your life. Own it and dethrone it.

Key Point #3: O=Offer your anger to God.

Read Genesis 4:6-8.

God saw Cain's anger and understood his pain. He lovingly reached out to Cain, assuring him he could be just as pleasing to God as Abel was; all Cain had to do was the right thing—he even offered Cain advice on how to do it. Cain was given the choice to do what was right and to be pleasing to God. Cain refused God's help and advice and chose to allow his anger to fester and

Keepin' It Real!

This would be a great time to share an incident from your own life when you made a right or wrong decision to control your anger, what the outcome was, and what you learned from the experience.

grow into a rage sufficient to murder his own brother in cold blood.

Just as God warned Cain, he warns us that sin is crouching at the doors of our hearts, waiting to devour us, and we must master it. Let's look at just how sin may be crouching at our hearts' doors.

Explosive Attitudes

Distribute copies of the "Explosive Attitudes" handout (p. 16). Have students form groups of three and take two or three minutes to read the handouts and compare their responses. Then lead a short discussion.

• Which of these attitudes do you think is potentially the most explosive? Why?

• What did this activity show you about anger?

Hold up the five-foot length of string.

This string represents our inner fuse—how long we can keep our cool. Each of the attitudes you just discussed has the potential to shorten our fuses and is an opening for sin that is crouching at our heart's door.

Read the first attitude, and snip a six-inch length from the string.

How is this a fuse-shortener and an opening for sinful anger?

Repeat this for each of the attitudes on the handout until you have no string left. As you can see, our human ability to keep our cool is limited. But with God… *(begin pulling the string from your other pocket)* our fuse can be unlimited. *Keep pulling string out of your pocket.* That's why we must offer our anger to God.

Key Point #4: L=Let others help.

God tried to save Cain from himself. He let Cain know that he had a choice. God would have been with Cain and would have helped him do what was right. But Cain would have none of that.

In the same way, God offers us resources to help us control our anger and develop as peace-makers. How does God help us control our anger? *Allow students to respond.*

God gives us the example of Jesus and how he kept his cool. He gives us his Holy Spirit as an unlimited resource of power, strength, and wisdom for controlling and overcoming our anger. He supplies us with teachers, parents, and good friends who can help us, counsel us, and advise us.

We must be willing to let others help us control our anger and to seek peace.

Keepin' It Real!

This is a great time to share with students how a mentor or peer helped you learn to control your anger.

Closing Challenge

To better control our anger or to uproot attitudes that can easily lead us to anger is not enough. We must also crucify our pride and selfishness, which provoke our explosive attitudes. We can do this by regularly and deliberately practicing kindness toward others. We must kill our inner anger with kindness.

The best way to do this is to strive to be kind in all of our dealings with others. Right emotions will follow our right actions. As we practice kindness, our hearts will be softened and we will not be as easily enticed to lose it with others or blow up.

Commitment Cores

Have students form groups of two or three to discuss these questions:

• Which comes easiest and most naturally to you, anger or kindness? Why?

• Why does God call us to practice kindness and seek peace when that can feel impossible to do sometimes?

• How do you need help controlling your anger? How can God help?

• What one thing will you do to better control your anger?

Have students pray for one another in their groups according to what each person has shared.

Cut six-inch lengths from your string. If you would like to commit your inner fuse, anger, or any other explosive attitudes to God, come and pick up one of these pieces of string. Keep it in your pocket throughout the week as a reminder that God is constantly with you. God is ready to give you all you need to have the unlimited ability to be a peacemaker in any and all situations you face.

Close with an appropriate prayer.

Reality Bite

Have a Christian counselor come to your group and offer solid advice on how to control anger and diffuse potentially violent real-life situations. Also consult a guidance counselor or administrator at a school near you to find out if your group members can provide a peer conflict-resolution service (a program in which students can help one another settle their differences peacefully). Most schools have access to all the training materials you would need to set up a successful peer conflict-resolution program.

Family Devotion Online!

See www.youthministry.com/family_devos for an activity-packed family devotion that you can download for free and copy for your students' parents.

Explosive Attitudes

Instructions: Get with two other people, and read the following list of attitudes together. As each attitude is read, each person should respond with "me" or "not me" to indicate whether or not the attitude applies to him or her. Take note of how many "me" responses each person gives. Afterward discuss with your small group what you think your responses indicate about you and your anger.

- **I have a hard time letting go of past hurts.**

- **I have to make my own way and look out for myself because no one else will.**

- **Turning the other cheek and walking away from a fight doesn't work.**

- **I watch violent or gory movies on TV or at the theater and have little to no emotional reaction.**

- **I become angry pretty quickly when I am embarrassed or if someone shows me disrespect.**

- **I am more likely to fight than to walk away from a fight, even if it's just verbal.**

- **Life really isn't fair.**

- **The pain and suffering of other people just doesn't get to me.**

- **Most people don't understand me and try to keep me down.**

- **When I get angry, I lose control and explode.**

Love: It's a Risky Business!

Topics

Loving the unlovable, reaching out, unselfish friendship

Scripture Base

Luke 10:25-37

The Point

We must freely share the unlimited love Christ has shown to us with those who seem unlovable.

Stuff You'll Need

TV and VCR; the movie *Dumb and Dumber* (New Line Cinema); big pictures (from magazines) of homeless people, starving children, AIDS-stricken people, currently popular movie stars, star athletes, and celebrities; poster board; glue sticks; copies of the "Good Sammy" skit on page 21

Preparation

Before the session, write the Commitment Cores questions on a chalkboard or a sheet of newsprint. Mount pictures of homeless people, starving children, AIDS-stricken people, movie stars, star athletes, and celebrities on separate pieces of poster board. Display these on the walls of your meeting area.

Introduction

Well, you won't believe it. I let the word out that we have an incredibly friendly group here, and all these people sent me their pictures so you would consider making them some of your best friends—people you would hang around with all the time, since they'll all be moving here soon. Choose one of these people to be your friend, but be sure to make your choice based on the same way you typically choose your friends.

Friendship Frenzy

Have each group member take one or two minutes to choose which picture to stand under. Standing under a picture indicates that the group member will accept that person's offer of friendship. When everyone has chosen a picture, lead a short discussion.

• Why did you choose who you chose? What do you look for in a friend?

• What would you gain if the person you chose was your best friend?

• Of all the people depicted, which of them would be riskiest or costliest for you to befriend? Why?

• Are you typically risky in your friendship choices? If so, how? Why?

If we're honest, we'll admit that we all look for certain types of people to be our friends.

Leadership Tip

Challenge students who choose to stand under the pictures of starving children, the homeless, or those with AIDS. Ask them, "So are you sure these are the friends you would typically choose?"

When people don't meet our standards, we typically don't get close to them. That would be a pretty risky business! Let's look at that risk for a moment.

Dumb and Dumber

To show an example of someone who is a risk to love, play a clip from Dumb and Dumber. *Begin the video at 1 hour, 31 minutes, 00 seconds when Lloyd professes his love to Mary. End the clip when Lloyd is excited because he has a "chance" at love with Mary.*

Looking for friends can be a problem for us as Christians because we're called to love everyone with an unconditional love without limits. Not only are we called to this, but God also has richly gifted each of us to love others without limit or condition—the same way he loves us. He showed that love by dying on the cross for us while we were still sinners. Believe it or not, God wants us to take the risk to love people we might normally overlook. Let's look at this risky love today.

The Message

Key Point #1: Risky love is a full-time job!

Christians are called to love without limit at all times. To learn more about this, let's look at a story about a good guy named Sammy.

Good Sammy

Enlist group members to play the following parts in the "Good Sammy" skit (p. 21): the traveler, robbers (one to three people), a priest, a Levite, Sammy, the innkeeper, and a donkey. Everyone else should make animal and nature noises. Have them simply act out their parts as you read the narration. Actions are in boldface, so pause for actors to perform them as you read. Feel free to have actors repeat an action if you feel they aren't hamming it up appropriately. When the skit is over, read Luke 10:25-29, summarize Luke 10:30-36, and read verse 37. Then lead a short discussion.

- What motivated Sammy to stop when others passed by?
- What set Sammy apart from most people?
- Jesus affirmed that to inherit eternal life we must love the Lord with everything in us and love our neighbors as ourselves. What do you think that means, and why do you think Jesus calls us to do it?

Love in its truest, purest form is not something we can limit, choose to give or withhold, control, sponge only for ourselves without sharing, or reserve only for those we feel deserve it. And as Christians, loving others is not something we are to turn on and off.

We're called to share love. If it's God's love, it's fully flowing all the time, regardless of where we are or who we're with. For us love is a full-time job—job one for the Christian!

Key Point #2: Risky love requires God!

In the Bible account we read earlier, the Samaritan must have needed God's help to love the injured and robbed Jewish traveler. Why? Because the Jews hated Samaritans, and the Samaritans hated the Jews. Jesus knew what he was doing when he told a parable about a *Samaritan* rescuing a *Jew*.

For a Samaritan to show such compassion and love to this beaten and robbed Jewish traveler was truly a work of God. The Samaritan had to do this with God's help.

In the same way, we need God's help to love without limit. Human love is so limited and selfish. Sometimes we need God to help us see others the way he does, to help us feel what he feels. That is the point of Christianity. We are God's ambassadors of love to this world!

Key Point #3: Risky love is gonna cost ya!

Think about what Sammy got out of this whole deal. First, caring for this beaten-down reject cost him time. It may have cost him friendships. If other Samaritans had seen him, they might have ridiculed him, rejected him, or tried to dissuade him from showing such compassion to a Jew. It cost him his comfort. The whole thing was very inconvenient. It cost him energy to fix up and haul the guy. It cost him money—he paid for the guy's medical, lodging, and food expenses. All this for a stranger! And for what?

Sammy got nothing in return! Or did he?

What do you think he received from all this? *Allow students to respond.* Somehow that was enough for him. Somehow that must be enough for us, too. Love is a risky business that will cost us. Just as Jesus paid the ultimate price of love for us and our souls, we are to love others unselfishly—without limit or condition.

No matter how you slice it, risky love is gonna cost ya!

Keepin' It Real!

Be sure to share with students a time you felt that God really helped you love someone who was hard to love. Remember to share the happy ending (if there was one).

Closing Challenge

There was a guy named Brian who was a little like the beaten man in the story of the Good Samaritan, but his story didn't have such a happy ending. Here's his story.

Tell group members the following true story.

Brian was a difficult child for other classmates to like. For one thing, he was overweight—an attribute that youngsters find difficult to accept in a peer. He also suffered from attention-deficit disorder. And though he displayed a lively sense of humor, Brian was also prone to interrupt conversations and become overexcited, often causing embarrassment to those around him. Yet he had such a tender heart. His mother described him as possessing "a keen sense of right and wrong," often feeling "frustrated by the cruelty and injustice he saw in the world."

Brian grew up in a loving family, but they had no idea how much he internalized the laughter and snickers of others. He just didn't talk about it. Instead, he seemed to extend forgiveness and freely grant the benefit of the doubt. Most of Brian's classmates didn't think much about it either. In the world of middle school madness, Brian didn't take up much space. A quiet, pudgy kid, he was sort of *out of sight, out of mind.*

That's why everyone was so shocked the day this fourteen-year-old came to school carrying a concealed weapon and, in the school cafeteria, ended his life by shooting himself. Perhaps he chose the cafeteria because it had come to symbolize so much of the torture he endured.

Days later, when his parents found some of his poetry, they began to understand the depth of pain Brian had internalized from years of relentless teasing, torment, and verbal abuse from peers. His writings speak for thousands:

For all my life I have lived with the words that haunt me. The words of America's sadistic children. Children who had been so distorted by the images of insult to all those who are "different" that they don't even have the capability to understand that what they do is wrong.

Although the light is wide in its spread, they still cannot see the pain on my face.

The pain that their eyes bring to bear when they look upon me.

They see me as an insignificant 'thing,' something to be traded, mangled and mocked.

You may search for us all your days, but never find us.

We are everywhere, yet we are nowhere.

Does the church have a message for kids like Brian? Might an embracing youth group have made a difference in his life? Sadly, he had never been invited to such a function. Might the story have ended differently if he had been? We will never know. Only one thing is for sure: Our schools and communities are filled with thousands more like Brian. (Excerpted from *Risk in Our Midst* by Dr. Scott Larson. Used by permission.)

Who will have the guts to risk loving someone like Brian? Who will look for that one lovable piece in unlovable people—that piece you can love with all your heart, like Brian's sense of humor— and let love grow from there? How far are we willing to go to love someone without limits?

Commitment Cores

Have students form groups of two or three to discuss these questions:

• How satisfied are you with how easily you show love to others?

• Without naming specific people, does Brian remind you of anyone? Why?

• Who could you be more of a friend to?

• What one thing will you do to reach out with love to that person?

Have students pray in their groups according to what was shared. Close by asking God to enable each student and adult leader to love without limits.

Extra Skit and Family Devotion Online!

See www.youthministry.com/family_devos for a skit to add to this message and an activity-packed family devotion that you can download for free and copy for your students' parents.

Good Sammy

(Loosely based on Luke 10:30-37)

Instructions: Simply read the narration below, and allow group members to act it out as you read.

One day a man was traveling down the road, **leaping and skipping merrily, whistling a happy tune.** Suddenly some robbers **leaped from atop a junk car, rolled out of the sewers,** and **jumped from behind some big dumpsters.** They **hissed and growled** at the man. Then they **hissed and growled** at him some more. The man **struck the Karate Kid position for the indefensible kick.** But the robbers **did a few professional wrestling moves** on him and **beat him up pretty bad, mussing his hair, giving him a noogie,** and **doing other bad things.** They **stole his clothes** and left him half-dead.

The man **lay on the ground, writhing in pain and crying out for his mom.** When a priest **galloped by on his imaginary camel,** the man was so relieved, but he couldn't move. **"Well," the priest said, "I'd love to stop, but I have some work to do in the temple."** He **called the church charity committee on his cellphone** to see if they could help, but his phone was on analog roam, and he didn't want to pay over-limit penalties, so he **galloped away on his camel** and left the man.

The man began **going into spasms, sitting up and lying back down over and over and over and over again.** Just then a Levite came **jogging by.** He saw the man but **kept jogging in place.** He was making good time on his run and feared soiling his hands on a man who looked like he might be dead, which would make him unclean, so **he jogged on.**

Just then a man named Sammy came **strutting up** with his donkey, **listening to his MP3,** playing his favorite songs, **dancing to the music, and doing his cool-dude walk.** When he saw the beaten man, **he felt really bad.** He **bopped over to the man** and **wrapped the man's wounds in bandages.** Then he **loaded the man on his donkey** and **delivered him to an inn** where he took care of him, **feeding him, dressing him, fixing his hair, and feeding him some more.** The next day he **strolled away, doing his cool-dude walk,** but not before **throwing some change** to the innkeeper and promising to pay whatever debt the man incurred.

3. Bad 'Tudes, Dark Moods, and Soul Food

Topics

Attitude, mood swings, positive influence

Scripture Base

Psalm 42:3-11; Proverbs 15:15; 2 Corinthians 3:2-3; Philippians 4:8

The Point

Our attitudes are really truly under our control, and through them we can greatly influence others for good or bad.

Stuff You'll Need

TV and VCR, the movie *Hope Floats* (20th Century Fox), newsprint, markers, tape, a watch with a timer

Preparation

Before the session, write the Commitment Cores questions on a chalkboard or a sheet of newsprint.

Introduction

Ever had one of those days?

Hope Floats

To depict a bad day, play a clip from Hope Floats. *Before showing this clip, explain that Bernice accidentally hit Deloris in the face with the ball while playing volleyball. Deloris has threatened to beat her up.*

Begin the clip at 56 minutes, 57 seconds when Bernice and Travis are walking out of the school together. End the clip at 1 hour, 00 minutes, 44 seconds with the shot of the house.

Pair up with one other person. Then tell your partner about the worst day you've recently had and how it affected your attitude and mood. If anyone helped or encouraged you that day as Bernice's mother helped her, tell about that as well. If no one encouraged you, say who you wish would have and how. *Allow students up to three minutes to share, then have volunteers share with the whole group some of what they told their partners.*

Today let's look at what to do about poor attitudes and bad moods.

The Message

Key Point #1: 'Tude and mood come from soul food!

Read Philippians 4:8 and Proverbs 15:15.

Our attitudes color our whole personalities. Our attitudes are fed by what we feed our souls. Now the old maxim is true: garbage in, garbage out. But it's *not* the whole truth because the following are also true: positive in, positive out; beauty in, beauty out; love in, love out; and confidence in, confidence out.

Many times we end up in a funk because we feed our souls a constant diet of dark junk. If we feed our souls a steady diet of moody, dark, negative, defeatist, hopeless thoughts, music, and media, let's not be surprised when negativity, hopelessness, and depression are the most natural things we feel. Let's not be shocked when these are the first things that come out at the slightest challenge in our lives.

Stop the junk and starve the funk! Say it with me: Stop the junk and starve the funk! Let's have a continual feast on the goodness of life.

Soul Food Slogans and Sayings

Have students form girl-guy pairs as much as possible. Distribute newsprint and markers to pairs. Challenge pairs to come up with their own soul food slogans by using "in, out" sayings such as "garbage in, garbage out" and "beauty in, beauty out" or rhyming sayings such as "Stop the junk and starve the funk!" After about two minutes, have pairs hang their slogans on the walls.

* Which of these slogans and sayings are you going to remember this week?

* What difference can feeding yourself some good, positive soul food make in your life?

Key Point #2: 'Tude and mood are a choice!

Lead a short discussion, asking these questions:

* How important is attitude? Why?

* How difficult is it to choose a different attitude? Why?

* How will staying in control of our attitudes benefit us?

Read or summarize Psalm 42:3-11.

The psalmist was overcome with sorrow; his tears were his "food day and night." He poured out his soul—this guy was overwhelmed. He described the depth of his pain. But at the end of the psalm, the psalmist made a triumphant and profound *choice*. Mustering up all that was in him, with the help of the Spirit of God, he boldly proclaimed and commanded his soul, "Put your hope in God, for I will yet praise him, my Savior and my God."

What can we learn from the psalmist? Go to God with the pain, and ask him to help you. Then do what he tells you to do. It may be a decision like the psalmist made. God may put someone on your heart to go talk to. He could also call you to serve or encourage someone else who's down. Let's look at a story about this.

Keepin' It Real!

Be bold! Tell students of a time you were your own worst enemy. Tell them of a time you talked yourself into a funk because you fed your soul a steady diet of moody, dark, negative, defeatist, hopeless thoughts.

Wayne's Rotten Day

Tell students the following story. Let them know they should immediately act out what you are about to read when you point to them. When you come to an action, sound effect, or boldface line, point to one or more students to act out the part. To make it easier to participate, have students stand up during the story.

It's Monday, 7:00 a.m. Wayne wakes up late and **falls out of bed,** ending up in **a very strange position on the floor.** It's raining **(make rain and thunderstorm noises),** so he just knows he's going to have a horrible **(say "horrible"),** no good **(say "no good"),** rotten **(say "rotten")** day. His brother, who is usually his ride and who always **calls him a loser in a laughing, snotty way,** has already left without him. Everything is horrible in Wayne's world.

At 7:30 a.m. Wayne can't find his favorite jersey. He **discovers it in one of his older brother's dirty clothes heaps, puts it on, sniffs the pits, and feels light-headed. It smells funky!** Can his life get any worse?

At 8:00 a.m. Wayne arrives at school and **gets a big smile** when he sees his girl-friend, Tamika. He tries to **walk in a cool way—but then trips.** Tamika **giggles and snorts, giggles and snorts again, and again.**

At 8:15 a.m. just before Wayne leaves Tamika, they **lean toward each other to kiss.** Wayne is on a high. But then **she sniffs, then sniffs again near his pits and backs away in horror, saying, "You stink like a wet dog!"** Then she leaves. Ouch, that hurts!

At 8:17 a.m. Wayne's English teacher **grabs him at the door** and **says to him in an English accent, "Thou art a sloth, vile man!"** and gives him a tardy. This day is going right down the sewer. But then he gets his test back from last week, so he **uses both hands to make an A on his forehead** and **goes around to several people, saying, "A plus, and the crowd goes wild!" and "Wayne with an A—tsssss, hot!"** He is on a high.

At 11:30 a.m. Wayne **walks like a cool dude** with Tamika at lunch because she is fine and **tosses her hair like she knows it,** and he is so proud to be with her. It's all good.

At 11:31 a.m. Wayne **drops his entire food tray and slips and falls in the food. Tamika walks on, tossing her hair.** This would be a low.

At 1:00 p.m. Wayne is in art class, **telling his boy about his favorite band, singing and rapping some of the lyrics.** He gets detention for talking. Low.

At 1:40 p.m. Wayne totally **dominates in basketball,** but then the **guy he's covering scores four straight baskets over him,** and **Wayne's friends call him "a punk for making us lose."** Again, this day just isn't right.

At 2:00 p.m. **he sees Tamika and they head toward each other to hug. Then she stops five feet from him, holding her nose, saying, "No way, uh-uh."** He forgot to take a shower after basketball—and he's still wearing the dirty jersey. He **smells the jersey and almost passes out. He yells out to Tamika, "Where's the love, baby? Please don't leave me, baby!"** This is a low. His day is totally in the sewer. As he **walks to his locker, he moans and groans about how bad it's been.**

At 2:05 p.m. **Sarita walks up to Wayne and asks, "Can we talk?"** Wayne **gives her a smile and a hug because they're good friends.** She tells him, "Hey, my parents, like, they're splitting up. Yesterday they dropped the bomb. And you know

Mom's got cancer. I've never thought my dad was like this. Two days ago I was happy; now I'm losing everything." Wayne talks to her **(pantomime)**, listens a lot, and **tells her, "Me and Tamika will be there for you. We'll be praying for you too."** After a minute, **Wayne and Sarita hug and walk home.** Later Wayne realizes he hasn't thought about his rotten day since talking with Sarita. He prays for her **(pantomime)**.

How many of you will agree that Wayne had a rotten day?

• Why can getting into someone else's problem help us forget our own?

• What are some other ways to cope with a bad day?

You know, I can easily imagine the psalmist "leading the procession to the house of God." He reached out to others rather than simmer in his suffering. So did Wayne. Often this will be the *choice* that God lays before us as well.

You're at the age of raging hormones and mercurial tides of emotion. You feel things so strongly. Your emotions and moods seem so natural and uncontrollable that you may doubt your power to control them. Great news—you can be in control! No matter what you think or how strongly you feel, you can improve your bad 'tudes and overcome your moods.

Key Point #3: 'Tude and mood are contagious!

Outlast Laugh

Have students pair up. Each pair should then find another pair and try to make that pair laugh. Pairs should flip coins to decide which pair will try first to make the other pair laugh. Set your timer and start. Students can do whatever they want in a two-minute period except blow on or touch the pair they're trying to make laugh. When both members of a pair have smiled (even for a second) or time is up, the first round of the game is finished. Have pairs switch roles and play again. Pairs win by refraining from smiling the longest. Keep time for foursomes to determine which pair caused the other to laugh first. Then lead a short discussion.

• Was this easy or hard for you? Why?

• Were you surprised that you caught the laughter of others as easily as you did? Explain.

• Share a time you laughed the hardest or a time you couldn't stop laughing.

Just as the positive attitude—happiness—was contagious in this activity, negative, harmful emotions can also be contagious and catching.

Read 2 Corinthians 3:2-3.

Just as the people Paul was addressing were like letters from Jesus, known and read by all, we, too, are letters. People read your life every day. What are they seeing? hearing? feeling? How can you use this for God? What are your attitudes and moods saying to other people about you? about God? Your attitude and mood communicate a lot about you. We need to be sure that what our "letters" say is pleasing to God and loving toward others.

Leadership Tip

You may be wondering, "But what about kids who are struggling with clinical depression? How careless can it be to say that attitude and mood are a choice?" Before the end of the message, you should mention to students that if they or someone they know is struggling with depression or sadness and just can't seem to shake it, there is help available for them. Remember that unless you have the degree and the license to counsel, your best way to help is to refer such struggling students to a qualified counselor.

Leadership Tip

If you have a small group, have students simply pair up and do the activity one-on-one.

Closing Challenge

Our attitudes and moods say so much about us. And when responsibly chosen, they can be such important tools to lead others to God and his love. Our attitude and mood are chosen and fueled by our soul food. If you want to change them today, you can—it's your choice.

Commitment Cores

Have students form groups of two or three to discuss these questions:

• What message does your life send that you are most proud of?

• What message do you think you send your parents by your attitudes and moods? other people your age? other key adults in your life?

• What one thing would you most like to change about your personality "color" (the color that's painted by your attitude and mood)?

• What one thing will you do to step toward this personality "re-coloring"?

Have students pray in their groups for one another according to what was shared. Then close by praying that students will do what is necessary to forge new attitudes and moods as God enables them.

Reality Bite

"Brainwash Tour"—Go out together and watch a movie that will positively feed your souls. Go to a Barnes & Noble, Borders, or some other bookstore with a coffee bar, and enjoy beverages while reading only materials that will positively feed your souls. Have fun committing to think and say only positive things, challenging anything that strays from being positive. Say any kind word or do any kind thing you can think of for the people you meet, such as the ticket-taker at the movie, the cashier at the concession stand, and others. During the course of the evening, discuss what needs to change in each of your lives to create real change in attitude, mood, and ultimately the "color" of each person's personality.

Family Devotion Online!

See www.youthministry.com/family_devos for an activity-packed family devotion that you can download for free and copy for your students' parents.

Topics

Premarital sex, marital intimacy, purity

Scripture Base

Genesis 39; 41:15-57; Proverbs 7:6-23; I Corinthians 6:15-20

The Point

Staying committed to sexual purity can save us from being used, abused, and confused as a result of premarital sex.

Stuff You'll Need

TV and VCR; the movie *Hope Floats* (20th Century Fox); newsprint and markers (if you have a small group) or an overhead projector, markers, and transparencies (if you have a large group); a stepladder with at least eight steps (preferably a ten-foot stepladder); eight sheets of poster board

Preparation

Before the session, find one guy and one girl to simply be hams and act out what you read during "The Higher You Fly—The Harder You Fall" Activator on page 29.

On two separate sheets of newsprint or on a single transparency, draw the illustration of the two circles shown below.

On separate sheets of poster board, write the following statements, using big letters and bright colors: "Eye contact with the dream guy or girl," "Cool date invitation," "Sweaty hand-holding," "Arm around shoulder," "The first kiss," "The mega kiss," "Getting all touchy-feely," and "Sexual intercourse." Set up the ladder in the meeting room, facing the side of the ladder toward the group. Attach the signs to the side of the ladder, starting with "Eye contact with the dream guy or girl" at the bottom and "Sexual intercourse" at the top. Place all the other signs between these two to show a progression.

Write the Commitment Cores questions on a chalkboard or a sheet of newsprint.

SEXUAL INTERCOURSE

GETTING ALL TOUCHY-FEELY

THE MEGA KISS

THE FIRST KISS

ARM AROUND SHOULDER

SWEATY HAND-HOLDING

COOL DATE INVITATION

EYE CONTACT WITH THE DREAM GUY OR GIRL

YES

NO

Introduction

Let's talk about sex! Anybody interested?

Have students pair up and discuss the questions "What one word would you use to describe how people at your school view sex?" and "What is the best reason you can think of to wait for sex until marriage?" Allow students a couple of minutes to share, then have volunteers share their thoughts with the group.

The whole sex issue can be really confusing at times. Because there are so many mixed messages out there, the temptation for premarital sex can be brutal. It's easy to give in and be used, abused, or confused because of those mixed messages. Let's look more closely at reasons to stay away from the danger.

The Message

Key Point #1: Don't be used!

Summarize Proverbs 7:6-23.

Just as the man was enticed by the woman calling out to him in the street, so we are enticed by voices, though often from different sources we probably don't think about too often. Let's talk about the voices that influence us to say yes and those that influence us to say no.

Yes or No

Let's consider some of the voices that tell us, "Yes, go ahead and have sex before marriage" and the voices that tell us, "No, you're safe and strong when you save sex for your husband or wife."

• What are some of the "voices" that tell you "yes," to just go ahead and have sex before marriage? *As students respond, write their responses on the newsprint or transparency near the "yes" circle. They may say things like "boyfriends or girlfriends who lack self-control or moral values," "movies," "pornography," "sexy advertising," and "friends."*

• What are some of the "voices" that tell you "no," to save sex for marriage? *As students respond, write on the newsprint or transparency near the "no" circle things like "parents," "the church," "Christian friends," "youth pastor," "Sunday school teacher," "Christian music," and "Christian books."*

• What are some possible motivations for the "yes" voices that urge you to have sex before marriage? *Write inside the "yes" circle things like "Sexy advertisers just want my money," "Sexually active friends want me to be like them," "Movie people want to entice me to see their movies," and "Music people want me to buy their records."*

If you had friends who were always trying to get your money and your stuff and who were constantly trying to get you to live below your high standards, you would consider them selfish users. They would be getting close to you to use you. And if such people claimed they loved you, why would they treat you like that? Beware of the selfish users out there.

• How would these friends qualify as users (people who use other people)?

• What are some possible motivations for the "no" voices that urge you to save sex for marriage? *Write inside the "no" circle things like "My parents love me," "My church wants me safe," and "My youth pastor wants me to have a strong relationship with God."*

As you can see, most of the "yes" voices are out to use you—wanting your money and stuff—while most of the "no" voices are motivated by love for you.

Don't be used. Be led by love as you work on saving sex for marriage.

Key Point #2: Refuse to be abused!

Ever suffered a heartbreak? There's nothing like it…

Hope Floats

To show a heartbreak of epic proportions, play a clip from Hope Floats. Begin the clip at 43 seconds as the movie begins with a tacky, tell-all TV show. End the clip at 4 minutes, 26 seconds with a close-up on Birdee.

Everybody say it with me—Ouch!

Read or summarize 1 Corinthians 6:15-20.

This passage speaks of the "joining" that occurs when two people engage in sex. This emotional bond is a strong one and isn't easily broken. When the breakup happens…well, let's just say it can hurt *really* bad.

Keepin' It Real!

Go ahead—tell them about your first, worst heartbreak. Remember, keep it real!

The Higher You Fly—The Harder You Fall

Draw attention to the ladder. Have the volunteer couple come forward along with a young or small member of your group who can be the climber in this illustration. You'll also need at least one adult to be a spotter for the climber.

Have the climber stand on the first step of the ladder, and have the couple stand by you to act out what you speak.

Stage 1: Eye contact with the dream guy or girl—Guy sees girl clear across the room, and she sees him. She flutters her eyes and thinks of her favorite ballad and sings it aloud. *Wait for girl to sing.* Guy starts to sweat and does a Tarzan call…*Wait for guy to do Tarzan yell.* If it all crashes and burns here, there's not a big sense of loss for our climber. *Shake the ladder pretty hard.*

Have the climber stand on the second step of the ladder, and have the couple stand about ten feet apart and act out what you speak.

Stage 2: Cool date invitation—Guy is feeling very suave. He knows he's looking good. She's feeling pretty fine too. He struts over, doing his totally cool-dude walk. She strikes a disaffected, nonchalant stance. "Hey baby," he says, "you and me could be good together."

And she's like, "Sure, here's my card, my cell number, my beeper, my best friend's cell, my best friend's beeper…"

Shake the ladder pretty hard. Still nothing too tough if it ends here.

Have the climber stand on the third step of the ladder, and have the couple stand by you and act as you speak.

Stage 3: Sweaty hand-holding—Well, here it is, the first date. The guy and girl are really nervous and not talking a whole lot, sputtering out broken phrases and sentence fragments. *Wait for couple to ad-lib some broken phrases and sentence fragments.* After the movie starts, he makes two failed attempts, sticking his hand in the Coke and then the popcorn. Finally, he finds her hand and holds it.

Shake the ladder pretty hard. Still not a whole lot of pain if it ends here, but there would be a little bit.

Have the climber stand on the fourth step of the ladder, and have the couple stand by you and act as you speak.

Stage 4: Arm around shoulder—Well, it's date two, and they're side-by-side in his ride. The guy puts his arm around the girl's shoulders. They're close, even sharing the same drink. She even burps, and they both just laugh. They sit and talk at a coffee shop, skipping the movie.

Shake the ladder pretty hard. They're coming together. It would be a downer if they parted ways now.

Have the climber stand on the fifth step of the ladder, and have the couple stand by you and act as you speak.

Stage 5: The first kiss—At the end of the night on the third date, he stands facing her at her front door. They have joined both hands. They make two failed attempts at their first kiss (he goes right, and she goes left; he goes left, she goes right, and they keep smacking heads instead of smacking lips). But then they find the target.

Shake the ladder pretty hard. If it ends now, it will hurt.

Have the climber stand on the sixth step of the ladder, and have the couple stand by you and act as you speak.

Stage 6: The mega kiss—OK, sometime later the guy and girl are alone in his car, fully embraced and involved in an amazing liplock. *Allow couple out of this if they hesitate—it will be just as funny. Feel free to intervene if they're too enthusiastic.*

Shake the ladder pretty hard. They're feeling really close—is it love? It will really hurt a lot if it ends here.

Have the climber stand on the seventh step of the ladder and ask the volunteer couple to take a seat.

Stage 7: Getting all touchy-feely—Now this is where our parental guidance kicks in, and don't even use your imagination for these next parts—not allowed. Well, gone are the movies, close friends, family, and cool talks…these two are just into each other, and the "dates" have turned into mostly make-out sessions with groping and so on. They feel deeply in love.

Shake the ladder pretty hard. A breakup at this point would be very painful and would result in crying and depression.

Have the climber stand on the eighth step of the ladder.

Stage 8: Sexual intercourse—Here it is, all the way. They're together at her house, and no one is around. Everything seems so perfect. They love each other so much. "This is my one and only, my soul mate." But then the breakup!

Shake the ladder pretty hard. A breakup at this point would be devastating. The guy and girl doubt if they'll ever love again. They contemplate dark options. They're overwhelmed with rejection, anger, pain, and wanting the other person back. They feel like a part of them has died.

Have students form pairs and discuss their biggest heartbreak, how they felt at the time, how they feel now, and what they learned from the experience.

Remember how much you cared for that person involved in your heartbreak? Maybe you still do. But it did end because 99.9999 percent of dating relationships end. If sex is involved when the breakup occurs, instead of parting ways, it feels more like being ripped and torn. The breakup is already tough enough. When sex gets into the scenario, it can be devastating.

Key Point #3: Save yourself from being confused!

Summarize the story of Potiphar's wife and Joseph in Genesis 39, then summarize Genesis 41:15-57, stressing the fact that Joseph was blessed by God.

Joseph didn't have *any* confusion about who to listen to when he faced temptation: Potiphar's wife or God? his own heart or the Spirit within him? He listened to God and managed to avoid a grave sin—and the judgment for that sin. Years later, God blessed Joseph richly for his righteousness.

Save yourself from being confused, learn God's voice, and obey God and all the others he has put in your life to help guide you into the best for your life.

Closing Challenge

Pre' or Marital Sex?

Read the following stories to students.

Pre'

Gregg and Jenny decide, "Hey, why wait for marriage? Everyone else is doing it, so why not us?" The sex is sneaky, occasionally in one of their homes but usually out in isolated places. It's filled with fear of disease, of pregnancy, of getting caught, of what their parents would think, and of what other Christians would think. It's clouded with guilt (they always feel so bad afterward). Sex has become bigger than anything else in the relationship (they don't just laugh, talk, and get to know each other in other ways like they used to). It pulls them further from others than ever (no one else can get in their "bubble"). It makes them feel very average (we're just like the non-Christians we know). It's confusing. Sometimes one or both want to get rid of the sexual activity, but they seem helpless to stop it, and that's scary for them.

• What can you add to this? What can you say about Gregg and Jenny's premarital sex in comparison to marital love?

• So why do so many people, even Christians, engage in sex before marriage?

• What would you do if Gregg or Jenny came to you for advice? Why?

Marital

Jordan and Clarisse thought, "Everybody else seems to be doing it, but we're not everybody else." They decided to be strong and commit to purity. They minimized their

Keepin' It Real!

If you're married, tastefully contrast for your students—in a personal way—the superiority of marital intimacy over premarital sex.

If you're single, tell students about your commitment to purity. Tell them what you do on dates to stay on track with that commitment and why.

time alone and hung around with others most of the time. They committed to unselfish things, like ministry to others, as part of their dates. They maintained their close friendships. They built lifelong relationships.

They kept getting to know each other, having long talks, and joking around with each other. Then they got married.

When they have sex now, they're consumed and transported to such a cool high because they're one—committed to each other for life. There is no fear, no sneakiness, no guilt, and no risk of sexual disease. A baby would only be an added blessing to their already full life. In the future they'll look their kids in the eyes when they talk about sex.

They were never deceived into thinking that sex was the basis of their relationship, the main part of their relationship. They aren't haunted by memories of past lovers or ashamed of their past—in fact, when they look back, they can see what a huge spiritual victory they won by staying pure.

• What can you add to this? What can you say about Jordan and Clarisse's marital love in comparison to premarital sex?

• So why should people, especially Christians, hold off on sex until marriage?

Commitment Cores

Have students form groups of two or three to discuss these questions:

• Which part of this message sticks out in your mind? Why?

• What do you think God thinks when people use sex to use people, abuse them, and confuse them?

• What are the best reasons to save sex for marriage?

• What one thing is the first thing to do to commit to purity?

Have students pray for one another in their groups, thanking God for the power to live pure lives. Close by praying that each person would reaffirm a commitment to sexual purity. Ask God to help them live pure lives.

After the prayer, let students know that you realize there is a chance that some of them may have already become sexually involved with someone. If they would like to talk to you about that and what they should do now, let them know you're available and you would love to help. Let them know that God offers them a path back to his perfect purpose and plan for their lives.

Extra Activity and Family Devotion Online!

See www.youthministry.com/family_devos for an extra activity to add to this message and an activity-packed family devotion that you can download for free and copy for your students' parents.

Reality Bite

For a companion message to this one, consider using "Real Sex—True Love Waiting" from the book *Shake & Bake Messages for Youth Ministry* by Dean Hawk and Jim Kochenburger (Group Publishing).

Go out on a group date together. Eat fast food, see a movie, then consider having coffee afterward and sitting and chatting. Sometime during the course of the evening, emphasize the benefits of group dates.

5. R-E-S-P-E-C-T

Topics

Respect, unity, commitment, love

Scripture Base

I Samuel 18:1-4; 20; Matthew 22:37-40

The Point

As Christians we are called to love and respect others.

Stuff You'll Need

TV and VCR, the movie *Austin Powers: International Man of Mystery* (New Line Cinema), newsprint, markers

Preparation

Before the session, write the Commitment Cores questions on a chalkboard or a sheet of newsprint.

Introduction

Today let's begin with a little mingling!

Mingle, Mingle, Mingle

Have all group members stand in the middle of the room. Explain that in a moment you'll say, "Mingle, mingle, mingle!" At that time everyone should mill around in the center of the room. When participants hear you call out a number, they should form hugging groups containing that number of people. Any group members who are left out and can't find a group of the correct number are eliminated from the game. Play several rounds, or play until you have only two players left. Then ask these questions:

• If you were eliminated, how did it feel to be treated so coldly (no one hugged you, so you were out)?

• How is this like what disrespect can do in a youth group? Explain.

Christianity is all about love. But some people just don't get it.

Austin Powers: International Man of Mystery

To illustrate disrespect, show a clip from the movie Austin Powers: International Man of Mystery. Begin the clip at I hour, 5 minutes, 45 seconds when Dr. Evil says, "You just don't get it." End the clip at I hour, 6 minutes, 15 seconds when Scott decides to remain silent.

For 160 more great video-clip ideas like this one, see Group's BlockBuster Movie Illustrations by Bryan Belknap.

In the body of Christ, the church, and this youth ministry, respect is not an option—it's an expectation and part of our calling in Christ to let love live through us. Let's look more closely at respect today.

The Message

Key Point #1: Jonathan was one in spirit with David.

Summarize 1 Samuel 18:1-4 and 1 Samuel 20. Then read 1 Samuel 18:1.

Jonathan and David were one in spirit. They based their friendship on commitment to God. They needed no other common ground as a foundation for their friendship.

We must be one in spirit with one another. Our friendships need only be based on our mutual commitment to God—and we must not withhold friendship from people who at first glance don't fit our "friendship profile."

We show respect for one another by being one in spirit with one another.

Key Point #2: Jonathan loved David as himself.

Read 1 Samuel 18:1.

Do you remember this charge from Christ in the New Testament: "Love your neighbor as yourself"? Jesus said we're to love the Lord our God with all our heart, soul, and mind and that we're to love our neighbors as ourselves. "All the Law and the Prophets hang on these two commandments" (Matthew 22:37-40).

We show respect to one another by loving one another as we love ourselves—that means with some real depth from the heart.

The War Is Over

Tell group members the following true story.

To say that Brad Pearson and his father did not get along was a huge understatement. In fact, they were at each other pretty much all the time. There were a lot of reasons for this, but basically Brad's father was a functioning alcoholic who knew only one way to communicate with Brad and his brothers and sisters—through yelling, hateful words, and hitting. He was a hard man.

Most nights Brad would lie awake as he heard his parents arguing, screaming, and threatening to leave. He'd feel the familiar knot in his stomach. After a while Brad realized that what was going on at his house wasn't going on at his friends' homes—where he tried to stay as much as possible. And the resentment started to grow.

Brad and his father "parted ways" when Brad started junior high. There had been too many embarrassing incidents in front of his friends, too many hurtful words, too much apologizing for his father, and too much pressure and pain. Brad checked out emotionally.

By high school Brad would say outright that he hated his father. There was no feeling. There was no respect. Brad's father would curse him, and Brad would curse back twice as hard. One time, in a fit of rage, Brad almost hit his father. It was total craziness.

Brad was loved into the church through a youth home Bible study and gave his life to Christ when he was nineteen. He remembers thinking even as he said a prayer committing his life to Christ, "This is so cool—but I am still not going to make it right with Dad." His hatred still burned—especially when his father blew up at him for committing his life to Christ.

Two weeks later, while sitting with friends and talking about the love of God, Brad knew he must make things right with his dad. "Where do I begin?" he thought. The next morning while praying, Brad got the idea to write his dad a letter. In short, the letter read…

Dad,

I just want you to know that the war between us is over. I surrender—maybe you win, and I lose. I don't know. I am just so tired of all the fighting and all the crap we put each other through. All I know is, I want my dad back.

I'm tired of being an enemy; I want to be a son to you.

I hope you'll forgive me for all the stupid things I've said and done to you. God has put a love in my heart for you that is unbelievable. It's the real deal.

You are a gift from God to me. God gave you to me to help me be a godly man. That means he is going to speak through you words of wisdom and guidance for me. I need to hear them from you. I have so much to learn from you. And I promise, Dad, that I will listen to you, honor you, and respect you from now on. God will help me. Pray for me.

Love,

Your son, Brad

Brad left the note on the steering wheel of his father's car and went back to his room to pray. If the note made his dad angry, Brad feared he would lose hope for both of them forever. He prayed hard.

He heard his dad leave the house without saying goodbye, which was their custom. He heard his dad open the car door and start the engine. After a long minute or two, the engine was switched off. Footsteps came down the hall. He heard a knock. Brad opened the door.

There stood his father, holding the note, a tear trickling down his cheek. "I've noticed a change in you, Brad," he said, "and I want you to forgive me." Brad started to cry. He hugged his dad—for the first time in over ten years. "I'm going to take seriously what you've asked me to do," his dad said.

This proved to be a turning point for Brad and his father. But it also inspired his brothers and sisters to be restored to his father as well.

Brad and his father still have some rocky times. But they embrace when they greet each other and when they say goodbye. They tell each other, "I love you." They have the utmost respect for each other. They honor and praise each other. To this day, though Brad's father still isn't a Christian, he prays for Brad and shares with him what he feels God may be saying.

Key Point #3: Jonathan honored David above himself.

Read 1 Samuel 18:3.

Jonathan was heir to the throne, and he humbled himself and established a covenant with David, who would be king instead! Jonathan honored David above himself. Jonathan and David did what they could to build each other up and to help each other succeed.

Honor Freeze Frames

Let's work together as a group to come up with some snapshots of "honoring" and ways to do it. *Have group members form five drama troupes. Assign each troupe one of these freeze-frame ideas: a teenager honoring a parent, a guy honoring his girlfriend, a guy honoring a loner everyone else rejects, a teenager honoring a teacher, and a girl honoring her friend. Allow each drama troupe to do a ten-second pantomime then its freeze frame for at least fifteen seconds. After all troupes have performed, ask:*

- What was easy or difficult about your freeze frame?
- What are some practical ways Christians can honor one another above themselves?

We must put the needs of other Christians before our own. We must look for ways to help one another succeed and find our dreams. We must encourage one another. We must build one another up in the eyes of others. We must serve one another in as many ways possible. We must honor one another above ourselves.

We show respect to one another by honoring one another above ourselves.

Key Point #4: Jonathan pledged openness and honesty to David.

Read 1 Samuel 18:4.

By laying the robe and tunic at David's feet, Jonathan was promising honesty, openness, and humility to David. No lies, no holding back, and no control games or power trips. They were going to communicate on the same level.

Respect calls us to stay away from the gossip and the rumor mill. It calls us away from the land of negativity and acid tongues that bring "death" to others rather than life. It calls us to speak life to one another, to build one another up, to affirm, to encourage, and to express love and commitment. We speak only truth.

We show respect by being open and honest with one another.

Key Point #5: Jonathan pledged to never harm and to always protect David.

Read 1 Samuel 18:3-4.

Jonathan laid down his sword, belt, and bow. He was pledging never to harm and always to protect David. He promised David that he would love him and never harm him by what he said and did.

We, too, must refuse to bring or allow harm to come to one another. We must stand up for fellow Christians who take tough stands and experience persecution. We must always hold one

---

another to the highest spiritual standards so that none of us will settle for lukewarm Christianity. We must build one another up with our words and actions.

We show respect by standing up for one another in persecution, protecting one another, and committing never to harm one another.

Closing Challenge

Respect Quiz and Respect Code

Read the following quiz statements to students, and have them rate your youth group on its respect level. If they strongly agree, they should stand up and applaud. If they agree, they should stand up and bow. If they disagree, they should slump down in their chairs with their arms folded.

• We do not use cut-downs, hurtful teasing, or mean-spirited humor.

• We don't clique up and exclude anyone—everyone feels "in" here.

• People feel safe here, like they can share their opinions and be honest and not worry about what people will think of them.

• In this youth ministry, the adult leaders respect the students.

• In this youth ministry, the students respect the adults.

• Everyone gets a lot of affection and gets really built up and encouraged from being here.

• There's a lot of love in our group.

• Our group has a very positive, upbeat atmosphere.

• We're becoming more like Jesus.

• We're kind, we're thoughtful, and we frequently serve one another.

• We could use a group hug right now.

Lead a short discussion.

• How do you feel after doing this quiz?

• Did you strongly disagree with everybody else on any statement? Why?

• What can we learn from this about our group and how to improve it?

Now's your chance to improve our group! *Across the top of a sheet of newsprint, write, "To be more respectful and loving to one another we must always..." Have students come up with some ideas of what the group must always do to be more respectful and loving, such as "Smile," "Treat new people like VIPs," and "Brag on one another."*

Across the top of another sheet of newsprint, write, "To be more respectful and loving to one another we must never..." Have students come up with some ideas of what the group must never do, such as "Put one another down" and "Ignore new people in the group."

After several minutes, display these newsprint posters for the group.

Commitment Cores

Have students form groups of two or three to discuss these questions:

• What's one way our group does the best job in showing one another respect? How do we not do so well in showing respect?

• Do you feel respected or disrespected here most of the time? Explain.

• How could you show more love or respect to others in the youth ministry?

• What one thing will you do differently from now on to show more love or respect to others?

Have students pray in their groups for one another according to what was shared. Then close the session in prayer, asking that each person be mindful and motivated to be loving and respectful (like Jonathan) at all times to all people who come into your group.

Reality Bite

Over the next thirteen weeks, have different group members present a two- to five-minute talk or activity at the beginning of each youth service on the following "respect" themes: Love one another (John 13:34), fellowship with one another (1 John 1:7), be at peace with one another (Mark 9:50), be devoted to one another (Romans 12:10), care for one another (1 Corinthians 12:25), serve one another (Galatians 5:13), forgive one another (Ephesians 4:32), be kind to one another (Ephesians 4:32), don't lie to one another (Colossians 3:9), encourage one another (1 Thessalonians 4:18), pray for one another (James 5:16), be subject to one another (1 Peter 5:5), and have compassion for one another (1 Peter 3:8).

6. The Servant's Life (It Ain't Flashy—But It's Real)

Topics

Serving, laying down our lives for others, sensitivity, kindness

Scripture Base

Matthew 20:26-28; 22:39b; John 15:12-13; Philippians 2:1-11

The Point

In Christ, as opposed to the world, the servant is greatest of all.

Stuff You'll Need

TV and VCR, the movie *Sister Act* (Touchstone Pictures), nails, tape

Preparation

Before the session, write the Commitment Cores questions on a chalkboard or a sheet of newsprint.

Introduction

Have students pair up. In our world, to most people, what makes someone truly great? Who is the greatest person now living (aside from Jesus)? *Have pairs discuss these questions for three minutes. When time is up, have students share some of their responses.* What makes someone great to God? *Have pairs discuss this for about two minutes.*

Jesus called the disciples together and said, "Whoever wants to become great among you must be your servant, and whoever wants to be first must be your slave—just as the Son of Man did not come to be served, but to serve, and to give his life as a ransom for many" (Matthew 20:26-28).

Jesus said this, so it's true, but it's so difficult to see how being a servant will lead to greatness of any kind, isn't it? In our world being proud, loud, ambitious, goal-driven, self-made, self-centered, highly motivated, powerful, and wealthy are the ways to greatness. Good news—God knows all about this struggle and will help us meet the challenge. Let's look at servanthood today and what it takes to be a servant from the heart.

> ### Leadership Tip
>
> Consider writing students' responses of Christlike and worldly greatness on a chalkboard or a sheet of newsprint to refer to throughout the session.

The Message

Key Point #1: The servant's heart

Let's take a little quiz to see how we rank as servants.

Servant 'Tude? *Highs*

After hearing each of the following statements, either extend a hand, which means, "That's me!" or fold your arms across your chest, which means, "Nope! That's not me!"

- Others compliment me on my servant attitudes or actions.
- I use my gifts and skills to serve my church.
- I use my gifts and skills to serve my family.
- Other people feel they can count on me when they need help.
- I make it a habit to help those in distress.
- When I see needy people or the homeless, it gets to me.
- The needs of others are at least as important as my own.
- I sometimes feel sad and ask, "God, why do you allow people to suffer?"
- Others compliment me on my sensitivity and love.
- I typically help people, even when it costs me time, cancels my plans, risks embarrassment, costs money, or even when their appearance repulses me.
- Friends say I am someone they can talk to about anything and that I'm always there when they need me.

#2

Have students turn to a partner and discuss the following questions. After a minute or two, have volunteers share their responses.

- What did this test tell you about yourself?
- How will you respond to what you learned?

Read Philippians 2:1-11.

In this passage God shows us two ways to live the life of the servant, as opposed to living a selfish life. First, we must consider others better than ourselves (verse 3). Second, we must look not only to our own interests but also to the interests of others (verse 4). We must stay alert to the needs of others and how to meet their needs.

Seeing Christ in the Poorest of the Poor

Check out this cool story of a journalist's encounter with Mother Teresa, which completely revolutionized his perspective on service and charity:

"She told a story of how one of the sisters had spent an entire day bathing the wounds of a dying beggar who was brought to them from the streets of Calcutta. Mother Teresa's voice dropped to a whisper as she told the hushed auditorium that, in reality, the nun had been bathing the wounds of Jesus.

She insisted that Christ tests the love of his followers by hiding in grotesque disguises to see if we can still see him.

A few nights later…a drunk accosted me. He was dirty and ragged and smelled bad. 'Did the bus leave yet?' he asked…

'You've missed it,' I told him. Then I thought about Mother Teresa…'C'mon, I'll drive you,' I said, hoping that he wouldn't throw up in the car.

He looked surprised, delighted and a little stunned…'Say,' he said, 'you must know me.'" (Excerpted from *Chicken Soup for the Christian Family Soul.*)

#3

The heart of the servant recognizes that when we serve and love others, we serve and love Christ. There are as many ministries and ways to serve as there are stars in the sky. There are nursing homes to visit, children who need sidewalk Sunday schools in their neighborhoods, elderly people who have homes in need of yard care, Sunday school classes that need to be taught, AIDS babies who need to be held and cuddled, camps that need to be run for special needs children, and so much more. The heart of the servant actively seeks to discover the needs of others and to meet those needs.

Key Point #2: The servant's choice

Read Philippians 2:6-7.

Jesus could have come to us as a conquering king, but he chose to come as a suffering servant. And he turned the world upside down by doing so. He made a daily choice to be a servant. He came to us in human flesh. He was fully God, but he was also fully human. Like us, he probably had to choose daily between dying to himself to serve others and being selfish and self-centered. He chose every time to be a servant. As we daily choose to die to ourselves to serve others, we find a whole new life—and we are forever changed.

Sister Act

To illustrate how living the life of a servant can bring us back to the heart of Christianity and refresh our faith, show a clip from Sister Act. Before playing this clip, let students know that the nuns in this movie have kept to themselves and haven't reached out to the community. They're locked in their routines, merely praying for those outside the walls.

Begin the clip at 58 minutes, 18 seconds, which shows the nuns standing outside a door as Sister Mary Clarence is being disciplined by the Reverend Mother for leading upbeat songs in worship. End the clip at 1 hour, 3 minutes, 50 seconds with Sister Mary Clarence trying to hide her face on television by holding up a child.

• What did the nuns' servanthood trigger in their church? their community? themselves? Why?

Those who want to be servants must choose servanthood over selfishness, selfish ambition, and self-centeredness. Right emotions follow right actions. As we continually make the choice to be servants, we'll steadily acquire the heart of the servant. Servanthood will become our nature and our passion; serving Christ will be our motivation.

Key Point #3: The servant's sacrifice

Read Philippians 2:7-8.

Serving is never convenient and always costs us something. Servanthood requires that we lay our lives down for others. We lay down our time, our money, our possessions, and our plans for others. This will kill our selfishness, our insensitivity toward people, and our spiritual coldness.

Nail Prints

Distribute nails to students. Have students press the sharp end of the nails against the palms of their hands or their wrists—just enough to feel some pain but not enough to risk penetrating *the skin. Have them do this while you read Matthew 22:39b and John 15:12-13 and lead a short discussion.*

- What sacrifices are you making right now by holding the nail?
- Jesus literally laid down his life for all of mankind. So what does he mean by asking us to lay down our lives for others? Why does he ask this?

Just as Christ's life was poured out to redeem mankind, he pours his life out through us when we serve, show kindness, and love others. Servanthood will kill what's in us that isn't like Jesus and will let his life, his nature, and his identity flow through us.

Key Point #4: The servant's glory

Read Philippians 2:8-11.

Jesus was glorified as a servant. He was exalted to the highest place. We, too, are exalted by God as we serve and bring glory to God by living our lives as servants.

Let's look at a story of how one man learned from what he suffered that the glory of the servant exceeds the glory of worldly success.

Jim Bakker, Ex-Con

Read the following true story to the group.

In the seventies and eighties, Jim Bakker was a well-known evangelist who experienced earthly glory. He preached a message of prosperity, insisting that God's people were to be rich. Through his PTL television show, he raised millions of dollars—promising people many blessings from God if they gave to his ministry. With some of the hundreds of millions of dollars he raised, he built Heritage USA, designed to be a showpiece Christian community. His personal fortune was mind-boggling. He had the finest of everything—and why not? All God's children deserved to live in high style, according to his gospel.

In the late eighties, Jim Bakker's world came crashing down as his adulterous relationship with a church secretary was revealed. He lost PTL and Heritage USA in 1989 when he was tried and convicted for mail and wire fraud for fundraising efforts at PTL. He served five years in prison.

By the time he was released, Jim Bakker had become an entirely different person. During his prison time, Jim Bakker, as a broken and humble man, spent his time studying the Bible and ministering to the broken men around him. Gone were the pride, the flashy persona, the slick talk, and the finery. Gone was the preaching of Christlikeness and wealth being one and the same. Jim has apologized profusely for the false gospel he preached for so many years. The key, he believes now, is simply to fall in love with Jesus.

After he got out of jail, Jim Bakker lived in the inner city of Los Angeles in a simple room at the Dream Center—a large outreach ministry. There he fed the hungry and ministered to drug addicts, prostitutes, the homeless, teenage runaways, and the other broken and needy people. In his current ministry of speaking in churches and ministering in the inner city, Jim Bakker feels more love and is happier than ever before.

Jim Bakker now experiences the glory of the servant—the deep soul satisfaction of serving others and being the heart and hands of Jesus extended to others. He's never been happier or more fulfilled. We, too, can know the glory of the servant as we serve.

Closing Challenge

The Christian life is one of loving, giving, and serving. He who is least is the greatest. The poorest is the richest. God is calling us to lay down our lives so we can live our lives out in service to others.

Distribute tape and one more nail to students. Have students use the tape to fashion their two nails into crosses as reminders of their calling to serve.

Commitment Cores

Have students form groups of two or three to discuss these questions:

• Who is the greatest servant you know? Why?

• How are you most like this person? least like this person?

• How might it change you to serve others consistently?

• What one thing will you do this evening to serve someone else? *Group members should help one another brainstorm ways to serve others.*

Have group members pray for one another in their groups according to what was shared. Pray that students will die to themselves daily so the life, love, and joy of Jesus can flow through them even more powerfully.

Reality Bite

With your group, tour a local homeless shelter, soup kitchen, charity, or other organization that reaches out to the poor and needy. Have volunteers from the organization tell about all the things they do to serve others. Ask why the people there do what they do day after day. It's best if you can involve students in some kind of service or ministry in the same visit. Afterward debrief with students and see who felt that tinge of joy and satisfaction that is a telltale sign of an emerging servant's heart.

Extra Movie Clip and Family Devotion Online!

See www.youthministry.com/family_devos for a movie-clip idea to add to this message and an activity-packed family devotion that you can download for free and copy for your students' parents.

7. Get Outta the Box! (God Has *Big* Plans for You!)

Topics

Gifts from God, God's plan for us, hope

Scripture Base

Jeremiah 29:11; Matthew 25:14-30

The Point

God has big plans for us and the future, and it all begins now.

Stuff You'll Need

TV and VCR, the movie *Mr. Holland's Opus* (Hollywood Pictures), five medium-sized boxes (barely sufficient for the average teenager to curl up inside), packaging tape, one small gift box wrapped with light-colored paper for each student or one copy of a gift box illustration for each student, markers, a mirror (the bigger the better), CD player, loud Christian music

Preparation

Before the session, wrap small gift boxes or photocopy a picture of a gift box. Heavily tape the medium-sized boxes except the tops, which should be open. Write the Commitment Cores questions on a chalkboard or a sheet of newsprint.

Introduction

Have students pair up. What's the wildest, coolest thing you've ever done for God? Allow students a minute or two to discuss this. After a couple of minutes, have volunteers share what they said to their partners.

You know what is often the worst enemy and the main thing that holds us back from doing some totally wild and cool things for God? These boxes!

Get Outta the Box!

Place the boxes in the middle of the floor. Have students take turns trying to curl up inside one of the boxes (after you try it yourself!). Just before they get in the boxes, teenagers should say the wildest, coolest things they can imagine God doing in their lives. Play some loud Christian music as students attempt to curl up inside the boxes. End the activity after two or three minutes, then lead a discussion.

• What do you think these boxes represent?

• What are some things that keep us boxed in and limit our ability to believe that God has big plans for us? Why?

• How should we respond to these things?

Leadership Tip

If your group is large, just have ten boxes up front, and have ten students come forward and do this as a demonstration.

Today we're going to demolish some boxes that have already begun to limit who we are becoming, some things that are threatening to keep our dreams small—things that are also making God seem limited and small in our lives.

The Message

Key Point #1: God's plan...to prosper you, not to harm you!

Read Jeremiah 29:11.

Can you believe God has something great for you? Big plans? To fully believe this, you have to stay out of the "wrong beliefs about God" box.

You've got to drop all those beliefs that tell you God is against you, that God doesn't want you to have fun, and that he dislikes most of the things you like and do. You've got to quit believing the lies that make you think that just being a teenager is sinful (everything you do, think, or say is bad or evil). Drop the thoughts that say God has the best stuff saved for others—never for you.

God, Almighty God, has big plans for you! He is crazy about you. God is your number one fan. He is so happy when you do the right thing or show his love to someone.

And when you blow it, God is eager to pick you up, dust you off, and get you back in the game. He is cheering you on every step of his road of righteousness. He loves all the wonderful stuff he has built into you—the talents, the personality, the dreams, the deepest heart desires, the aspirations, and the skills. He desires for these gifts to prosper inside of you. God has big plans for you—to prosper you and not to harm you. One proof of this is the unique gifts he has given you—gifts that are hard to see when you're not looking.

Mr. Holland's Opus

To illustrate the struggle sometimes involved in finding giftedness, show a clip from the movie Mr. Holland's Opus. Begin the clip at 19 minutes, 45 seconds when Mr. Holland tells Miss Lang to stop practicing. The clip ends at 21 minutes, 30 seconds when Miss Lang leaves.

For over 160 more great video-clip ideas like this one, see Group's BlockBuster Movie Illustrations, by Bryan Belknap.

- What was distracting this girl from seeing her own giftedness?
- How was she in a box?

Let's help identify and celebrate one another's giftedness right now.

Precious Gifts

Distribute markers and wrapped gift boxes or pictures of a wrapped gift box. Have students write their names on their gift boxes. Then have students pass their gift boxes around to others. Encourage everyone to write on each box that person's gifts, such as skills, talents, abilities, spiritual giftedness, unique sensitivities, things that they're knowledgeable about, and so on. You may want to display the gifts from 1 Corinthians 12 and Romans 12:5-13 where everyone can see them. Teenagers should leave two panels of each box totally blank.

Leadership Tip

If some students are new, they should write their gifts on their own boxes and pass them around for others to see. Interview these students, asking them to tell you everything they like most about themselves.

After a few minutes, have students write on one another's boxes ways they consider people to be gifts to them, to the church, or to the youth ministry. After several minutes, have students collect their gift boxes and spend some private time reading what everyone wrote, then lead a short discussion.

• What was the most meaningful thing written on your box? Why?

• What was written on your box that most surprised you? Why?

God has big plans for you, not to harm you, but to bless you and prosper you. What people wrote on your box are just a few precious gems. God has a whole treasure chest of good things for you.

Key Point #2: God's plan...to give you hope!

Read Jeremiah 29:11.

God wants you to fully know his plans for you so those plans can bring you hope. It's easier to go through the dark tunnels of life when you see the light at the end of them. His plans for you and his will for you are to be that light. To experience this, you have to stay out of the "bad stuff about me" box.

This box contains all the pain you've suffered; the bad things about you; the bad things others have done to you; and your weaknesses, failures, and mistakes. Unless these are given to God, they can eat your soul and rob you of your heart's joy, stealing your ability to believe good will come of your life. They will undermine your confidence and belief in yourself. They will make you doubt good things others say about you. Let's look at a story of one young man and his struggle to find hope.

Chris Zorich

Raised in poverty, born of an interracial union, raised by his single mother when his father left, living in the projects, beaten by other kids almost daily because of his racial mix, foraging in dumpsters with his mother—Chris Zorich thought his future couldn't have seemed more bleak.

Chris typically had no one to play with, so his mother, Zora, would throw the football with him, even as passing boys taunted. When he felt no love from anyone else in the world, his mother's love sustained him. Zora remained strong and resolute through every hardship they faced together and became a source of undying hope for Chris. As hostile as the world was, Zora always challenged her son to treat others like they were family, a lesson he never forgot.

When a high school coach sized him up as a football player and got him to play, things turned around for Chris. He went on to be a star player in high school and at Notre Dame. Zora died the night of Chris' last college football game, so she never got to see her legacy fully lived out through him.

He was drafted by the Chicago Bears and played in the NFL for several years, finishing his football career with the Washington Redskins.

Chris now attends law school and operates several organizations that function to feed hungry families, encourage kids to stay in school, finance a Notre Dame education for poor students who show promise, and take inner city kids to cultural events such as ice shows. He works hard to give kids a chance and a hopeful future.

Give that "bad stuff about me" box to God. Let him destroy it. Find hope in God. He is right

Keepin' It Real!

Be brave. Tell students how the bad stuff that happened in your life threatened to hold you back from what God had planned for you.

here for you and able to bring you hope no matter what you've suffered, no matter what bad things have happened to you. What's past is past; what's done is over. God has plans to bring you hope.

Key Point #3: God's plan...to give you a future!

Read Jeremiah 29:11.

God has entrusted tremendous gifts to you and has expectations for you right now that will determine what he will entrust to you in the future. But the box you have to stay out of in order to have this hope is the "what I'm doing today has nothing to do with my future" box.

Your future has already begun. I don't care if you're just flipping burgers—doing it well has lifelong benefits. What can you learn from flipping burgers that can help you succeed in the future? *Have students respond with things like "the importance of being punctual," "how to do laundry since I'm not allowed to mix my uniform with other clothes," "teamwork," "any job well done is worth it and something people will pay for."* You can take those few lessons—what you hate and love about any job— and start your own business and become a millionaire.

To have hope and enter fully into God's plan for you and your area of giftedness, you must consciously and with great effort identify and faithfully live out your giftedness now, however you can. If people say you are the most encouraging person in the world, encourage your brains out. If you are great with computers, learn everything you can about them and become an expert. Let's look in the mirror at your future.

Mirror, Mirror on the Wall...

Have students take turns looking at themselves in the mirror for ten seconds then completing this statement about the future: "I see someone who..." (For example, someone might say, "I see someone who...loves little children and could be a great pediatric nurse" or "I see someone who...loves to work with his hands and build and would be a great home builder.") When everyone has looked in the mirror, lead a discussion.

- What did you learn about yourself just now?
- What are you doing now to be who you want to be in the future?
- How do you feel, knowing God has a future for you?

Summarize Matthew 25:14-30.

As you're faithful in exercising your giftedness, God will steadily reveal to you your future, entrust you with more, and open up new areas of giftedness. God has a future planned for you that you'll love. Live it now!

Closing Challenge

You must seize God's plan for your life. As William Jennings Bryan once said, "Destiny is not a matter of chance, but of choice, not something to wish for, but to attain."

Play the music. Right now smash these boxes you tried to get in earlier—tear them up. Destroy these limitations on your dreams and beliefs about being all you can be. They represent your wrong beliefs about God, bad things that have happened to you, and your failure to see that your future is in your hands to build right now. *Allow students time to do this.* Move this stuff out of the way!

Have each person pick up a piece of cardboard and write on it, "Jeremiah 29:11—'For I know the plans I have for you,' declares the Lord, 'plans to prosper you and not to harm you, plans to give you hope and a future.'"

Commitment Cores

Have students form groups of two or three to discuss these questions:

• What is the biggest thing you got out of today's session? Why?

• When did you last use your giftedness?

• What are some ways you can use your giftedness at our church? in this youth ministry? Help one another brainstorm ideas.

• What one thing will you do tomorrow to use your giftedness to minister to someone else?

Close by having students pray for one another in their groups according to what was shared. Then close your session by asking God to open teenagers' eyes to their giftedness and God's great plans for them. Ask that their faith and hope carry them into God's best for each of their lives.

Reality Bite

Have motivated students read *An Enemy Called Average* by John Mason. This inspirational book will help your students dream and believe God has big plans for their lives. Discuss your thoughts and reactions to a chapter each week with students.

Family Devotion Online!

See www.youthministry.com/family_devos for an activity-packed family devotion that you can download for free and copy for your students' parents.

8. Developing an Unsinkable Faith

Topics

Developing tough faith, dealing with doubt, what faith is

Scripture Base

Genesis 15:6; Job 1:13-22; 2:7-13; 42:1-6; Matthew 8:5-10, 13; 9:1-8, 20-22; 14:25-31; Hebrews 11:1, 6, 11; 1 Peter 1:3-10

The Point

Faith can be toughened through doubt and even through crushing adversity if we keep our focus on Jesus.

Stuff You'll Need

TV and VCR, the movies *Titanic* (Paramount Pictures) and *Patch Adams* (Universal Pictures), five items that students will touch to recognize (such as a small statue or trophy, a printer cartridge, a novelty candy machine, a hand-held lawn-sprinkler gun, a battery charger, or whatever you choose) index cards, pencils, five boxes or paper sacks

Preparation

Before the session, write the Commitment Cores questions on a chalkboard or a sheet of newsprint. Place the five items into separate boxes or paper sacks. Leave a couple of them empty if you'd like. Number the bags or boxes from one to five, and place them on a table at the front of the meeting area.

Introduction

Some people have weak faith. They have a bad hair day and conclude God has turned his back on them. When they don't have a prayer answered as they asked, they're ready to give up on God. They fall into sin and run away from God rather than run into his arms. Turn to a partner, and share the coolest thing God has done for you. Then share a time you felt that God didn't quite come through for you as you had hoped. *Allow students up to three minutes to share, then have a few volunteers share their thoughts with the whole group.*

Let's look at some of what it takes to develop an unsinkable faith.

The Message

Key Point #1: Faith is faith, not fact.

Faith or Fact?

Distribute index cards and pencils to students. Have them number down the sides of their cards from one to four. Direct students' attention to the five bags or boxes on the table at the

front of the meeting area. Have students form five groups, and then have each group line up in front of one of the items on the table. Groups should guess their items without touching the items or bags or boxes or looking in them—if, in fact, there is anything in them—and write their guesses on their index cards beside number one. Ask:

• Are you exercising faith right now?

Tell them they have a choice whether or not to believe you, and insist that there is something in each of the boxes or bags—but act sly about it. Students should write "yes" (I believe you) or "no" (I don't believe you) beside number two on their index cards.

• How are you exercising or not exercising faith right now?

Now have each person reach into his or her group's box or bag and touch the item for ten seconds. Each person should use only his or her thumb. Then, next to number three on their cards, students should write what they think they just touched.

• Think about what you just wrote. Did you make your choice based on faith or on facts you discovered?

Pull the item out of each box or bag, and have group members see how well they did.

• What role did faith play in this activity? facts?

• What is faith? Work with a partner to come up with a way to describe faith to someone who doesn't go to church, and write it on your card next to number four.

After about two minutes, have several pairs share what they wrote.

Read Hebrews 11:1, 6, 11 and Genesis 15:6.

Having final, irrefutable, and convincing proof of something means you know it as fact—this isn't the same as faith. "Faith is being sure of what we hope for and certain of what we do not see" (Hebrews 11:1). Faith is a belief one holds that is without final, irrefutable, convincing proof. Faith doesn't demand answers but trusts in God when things don't make sense and answers aren't apparent.

Key Point #2: Faith is a risk.

Titanic

To show how faith can be a risk, play a clip from Titanic. Begin the video at 2 hours, 5 minutes, 25 seconds when Rose swims toward the room where Jack is imprisoned, handcuffed to a pipe. End the clip at 2 hours, 6 minutes, 32 seconds when Jack says, "I believe in you" and Rose breaks the handcuffs with an ax. Then lead a short discussion.

• How were Rose's actions a risk?

• How is faith risky?

• How has faith been risky for you, and why was it worth it?

Read Matthew 8:5-10, 13; 9:1-8, 20-22.

The nature of faith involves a risk. It's pretty risky to step out and stand in your faith, especially when everything is going wrong. Faith is a risk.

Keepin' It Real!

Share with students something you did that exercised risky faith and how your faith grew or was toughened as a result.

Key Point #3: Faith can be fueled by doubt.

Patch Adams

To make a point about faith and doubt, play a clip from Patch Adams. *To set up the clip, tell students that Patch learned that his girlfriend, Carin, was abused as a child and truly hated men as a result. Patch was the first man she trusted. When a mentally troubled patient called Patch's clinic, asking for help, Carin responded and went to the man's home to help. He killed her and then himself.*

Begin the video at 1 hour, 27 minutes, 44 seconds with Patch standing behind a tree. End the clip at 1 hour, 35 minutes, 5 seconds with Patch walking down a hospital hallway.

- What do you think Patch is thinking and feeling in this clip?
- How do you think seeing the butterfly restored Patch's faith?

Just as Patch's faith was restored when he noticed the butterfly, our faith will be restored when shaken if we stay focused on Jesus.

Read Matthew 14:25-31.

Doubt can fuel our faith if we're focused on Jesus. Look at what happened to Peter when he took his eyes off Jesus. He sank like a rock when he had been walking on water. He lost focus. If unchallenged doubts take root in us and distract us from focusing on Christ, the flame of our faith can actually be weakened or even extinguished.

Muscle Teach

Have students pair up and feel each other's unflexed biceps. Then have them take turns doing as many push-ups as possible. When students have done their last push-ups and are back in the "up" position (still in push-up position with arms extended), have their partners feel their biceps again. When both partners have finished, lead a short discussion.

- What were your partner's muscles like before push-ups? after push-ups?
- Why do muscles do this?
- How does putting dynamic tension on muscles cause them to grow?
- How can hard times and doubts build our faith?

Just as dynamic tension causes muscles to stretch and grow bigger as muscle cells multiply, hard times and doubts—when we trust in God and focus on Jesus—can be used by God to make us spiritually stronger with a tougher and more steadfast, trusting faith. To do this we must believe he'll be with us and he'll see us through—no matter how we feel. We should seek Scripture promises of God that we can stand on. We should talk to mature Christians who can tell us how God helped them through doubts and hard times so our own hearts will be encouraged. As we stand in our faith, it grows tougher and stronger.

Keepin' It Real!

Share with students a time you went through a tough bout with doubt, how you got through it, and how it helped your faith grow or toughen.

When we're focused on Christ, we can process doubt in a positive way. If we're distracted from Christ and lose focus on him, our doubts and hardships can weaken our faith. If we keep our hope in him and trust him to be with us, giving us joy and strength, doubt can actually fuel the fire of our faith.

Key Point #4: Faith must sometimes "die" and be "reborn."

Summarize Job 1:13-22; 2:7-13; 42:1-6.

Though he lost everything but his health and his wife, we see in Job 1:21 that Job worshipped God: "Naked I came from my mother's womb, and naked I will depart. The Lord gave and the Lord has taken away; may the name of the Lord be praised." Then he lost his health and was covered head to toe with painful sores. His wife encouraged him to curse God and die. In Job 2:10 he replied, "You are talking like a foolish woman. Shall we accept good from God, and not trouble?"

Ultimately Job's faith was completely changed by what he suffered. In Job 42:5-6 he said, "My ears had heard of you but now my eyes have seen you. Therefore I despise myself and repent in dust and ashes."

Sometimes faith even "dies" in a way. Many of us encounter times we suddenly never look at our faith quite the same again. Times when some tragedy or totally bizarre or unexpected thing happens. We lose our simple faith to find a more mature faith.

One modern example of this is in the life of Elie Wiesel.

When Faith Dies

Tell students the following true story.

Even as a young teenager, Elie Wiesel had an unusual interest in the things of God. He sought God earnestly, until, over the course of several months, the life of this young, religious teenager was shattered beyond description.

Elie and his family, like so many Jews during World War II, were rounded up like cattle, stripped of all dignity, and shipped off to a Nazi death camp. After his family was separated, beaten, and stripped of their clothing, came an unimaginable horror. Elie's mother and sister were marched away immediately to be thrown with thousands of others into a huge furnace.

Elie recounts, "Never shall I forget those moments which murdered my God and my soul and turned my dreams to dust. Never shall I forget these things, even if I am condemned to live as long as God Himself. Never" (excerpted from *Night* by Elie Wiesel).

As a result of the horror he experienced, Elie's simple faith died in that prison camp.

Read or summarize 1 Peter 1:3-10.

Faith can sometimes seem to die. But if we keep our hearts turned to God and cling to whatever hope we can find during those times, letting him carry the pain, we can see a wonderful, miraculous rebirth of our faith. A tougher, stronger, more refined, steadfast faith will be born.

Closing Challenge

Faith isn't faith until it's tested—that's the only time we can really be sure if we have it. And all faith must be refined and rid of all impurities. At times when everything goes bad, it's good to have a fully constructed fortress of faith. This is built simply by thinking deeply of all the ways God has been faithful to you, given you strength and direction in the hard times, led you to be a Christian, changed you, given you peace, and given you spiritual gifts—anything that shows how God has been faithful to you. When the roof caves in or your world falls apart, remember these things and fill your heart and mind with them as a hedge against doubt and unbelief. Face the fire, and your faith will be unsinkable.

Commitment Cores

Have students form groups of two or three to discuss these questions:

• What are two ways God has been faithful and good to you?

• How has your view of God changed since you were a child?

• What are some things that really tend to shake or weaken the faith of people your age? Why?

• Tell of a time your faith was shaken. What happened, and how did your faith grow stronger as a result?

• What one thing will you do in the future to be sure to emerge from doubt and adversity with a stronger, more mature faith?

Have students pray in their groups according to what was shared. Close with an appropriate prayer, asking that you and your students will be gutsy in the face of doubt and adversity and will develop an unsinkable faith that draws you closer to God.

Extra Movie Clip and Family Devotion Online!

See www.youthministry.com/family_devos for a movie-clip idea to add to this message and an activity-packed family devotion that you can download for free and copy for your students' parents.

Reality Bite

Have group members create simple pocket-size "Faith in the Fire" booklets they can use or share with others who might be going through a real test or trial. Motivated students can work together using concordances and study sections of Bibles, such as the index of a *Life Application Bible* (Tyndale House Publishers). This booklet can help struggling students stay focused on God in the midst of some typical teenage struggles that could harm their faith. Here are some ideas to get students started:

Disappointment—Psalms 13 and 20

Failure—Psalm 119:33-40

Feelings of depression—Psalms 16 and 119:169-176

Gossip about you—Psalm 31:19-24

Loneliness—Psalm 25:16-22

Mistreatment by friends—Psalms 3 and 9

Persecution—Psalms 14 and 21:7-13

Seemingly unanswered prayer—Psalm 13

Sin—Psalms 32 and 51

9. But Enough About Me... What Do You Think of Me?

Topics

Self-centeredness, sensitivity to others, love

Scripture Base

Matthew 22:34-39; Galatians 5:19-23

The Point

To find true joy and fulfillment in life, we must use deliberate, forceful efforts to get out of ourselves and into God and others.

Stuff You'll Need

TV and VCR, the movie *Hope Floats* (20th Century Fox), newsprint and markers (or an overhead projector, markers, and transparency), masking tape, paper, pens

Preparation

Before the session, write the Commitment Cores questions on a chalkboard or a sheet of newsprint.

Introduction

Remember the old acronym "J.O.Y."? J.O.Y. equals Jesus, Others, and You. What do you think this means? *Encourage response.*

Turn to a partner. Without mentioning names, take turns describing people who are like, "But enough about me...what do you think of me?" and who are totally into themselves. Describe what it's like to hang with them. *Allow students a couple of minutes to do this. Then have a few volunteers tell about their self-consumed friends—without naming names or revealing the identities of who they're talking about.*

Line 'Em Up!

Use masking tape to make two parallel lines on the floor of your room, ten inches apart. Students should stand between the lines. Have students stand in order according to what you say. Let them know they can't step outside the lines as they reorder.

Have students order themselves alphabetically according to birth month or street name, numerically according to shoe size or birth date, and in groups according to favorite food or color. Each time, they're allowed sixty seconds to get in order. After a few rounds of this, lead a short discussion.

• How important was cooperation in this game? selflessness?

• How important is selflessness to succeed in our culture? to succeed as a Christian? Explain.

Just as selflessness was important in this game, it is also important in our Christian lives. In our culture there seem to be no limits to selfishness and insensitivity to others. New lows in both categories are achieved daily. As Christians we're not to ride the selfishness express. We've been called to counteract the culture with selflessness, love, kindness, and giving. Let's look at that today.

The Message

Key Point #1: We must tear away from ourselves!

Read Galatians 5:19-23.

Circle "selfish ambition" in verse 20, but keep in mind that selfishness is a part of each act mentioned in this list. Selfishness is a big deal in our country, but this is nothing new. By ourselves we're all selfish and self-consumed.

Fortunately, as Christians we're given a new nature that's like God's nature. We have unlimited resources available to us in that nature to become truly loving, selfless, caring, giving, and kind people. But this kind of change can sometimes require radical steps like forcing ourselves to set aggressive goals for serving and expressing selfless love to others. In fact, let's practice this right now.

Selfless-a-thon!

Have students form teams of up to five people each. Distribute paper and pens to each team, and have them come up with as many ways to be selfless with one another as possible in three minutes, using just your room and whatever materials are there. For example, a team might mention giving someone a massage or sharing a kind word. Teams must perform the acts for one another as they list them. When time is up, create a master list on newsprint or an overhead transparency. When you've displayed the list for each team, have students give one another a round of applause.

- *What does this show you about our ability to be selfless? Explain.*

- *If you thought like this all the time—you know, "What can I do for those around me?"—how would it affect your relationships? How would it change you?*

As we do these right actions more and more, we'll notice right attitudes being born, attitudes that are tremendously stoked by serving and giving to others. So the payoff is worth it. To break the hold of selfishness on our lives, we must tear away from ourselves.

Key Point #2: Love the Lord your God with everything in you.

Read Matthew 22:34-38.

Why do you think this is the greatest commandment? God is basically telling us to love him with all our guts. Everything in us should be pointed at God and intent on pleasing, serving, and loving him.

This is not too much to ask. God has handcrafted each one of us, breathed life into us, and plotted our destinies. God stands ready to speak to us and guide us at all times. It doesn't seem too much to ask that we live to please him. Besides, even if he did nothing for us—didn't guide us or wasn't present in our lives—he still deserves our worship and our living to please him. We should live to please him simply because he's God and he inherently deserves our full devotion.

So what are some ways we can express love to the Lord? *List these on a chalkboard or a piece of newsprint. Have students explain their answers.*

We must love the Lord with all that is in us all the time in as many different ways as possible! To break the hold of selfishness on our lives, we must love the Lord our God with everything that is in us.

Key Point #3: Love your neighbor as yourself.

Read Matthew 22:35-39.

How is "Love your neighbor as yourself" like the first and greatest commandment? It's significant that when asked which was the greatest commandment, Jesus didn't stop at just one commandment but brought in another and forever intertwined the two—we can't have one without the other no matter what you think, no matter what you claim. If you say you love God—let me see your love for people. If you say you are someone who loves people—let me see your love for God! We can't truly love one without loving the other.

To break the hold of selfishness on our lives, we must love our neighbors as ourselves. Here's an example of one man who got this whole love thing right.

Keepin' It Real!

Tell students a personal story of a time someone showed you huge love when you desperately needed it.

Hope Floats

To make a point about being sensitive to the needs of others, play a clip from the movie Hope Floats. It's important to share with students some background to this clip in case they didn't see the movie. This scene takes place after Birdee's husband and best friend tell her on national TV that they are having an affair. Her husband leaves her, and Birdee, devastated, returns to her hometown. Birdee visits her father, who has Alzheimer's disease and lives in a nursing home. This is a clip of that visit.

Begin the clip at 39 minutes, 50 seconds when Birdee walks into her father's room. End the clip at 43 minutes, 51 seconds with a close-up on a snow globe.

Closing Challenge

Jesus went on to say that all the Law and the Prophets hang on these two commandments: to love God with everything in us and to love our neighbors as ourselves. To love like this is a tall order, but with Jesus in our hearts and a spirit filled with God's power to help us along, we can do it. Let me tell you about a young man who understands this whole selflessness and love thing.

Ian Thorpe

Ian Thorpe, an Australian swimmer known as the "Thorpedo," won three gold medals and a silver at the 2000 Sydney Olympics and proved to be one of the best swimmers in the world. Though acclaimed as a superstar and hero in his native Australia for years, there is more gold to this young man than gold medals.

Just a few years ago, when a friend named Michael Williams battled a form of cancer called non-Hodgkin's lymphoma, Ian was there every grueling step of the way, giving an encouraging word, designer clothes, the latest PlayStation game, or a nickname ("Uncle

Fester") to bring a smile to Michael's disease-ravaged face. After seeing Michael successfully beat his disease, Ian was incredibly inspired by Michael's courage and found new resources within to be the best he could be.

Ian Thorpe has proven to be a champion not just in the sport of swimming but a champion of selflessness and kindness—a genuine hero.

For Ian Thorpe, no matter what the accolades were, it was not about him. It was about others, especially his friend Michael. Selfishness is such a strong trap that we must make deliberate, forceful efforts in our lives to get out of ourselves and into others. But it's worth it.

Commitment Cores

Have students form groups of two or three to discuss these questions:

• Who is the most selfless, giving, thoughtful, loving person you know? Explain.

• What is the kindest, most loving thing someone has done for you recently?

• Does your kindness and selflessness deserve a gold? a silver? a bronze? no medal?

• What one thing can you do to tear away from yourself and be immediately more selfless, loving, and caring?

Have students pray for one another within their groups according to what was shared. Close the session by asking God to help each person in your ministry become radically, immediately, and consistently selfless and loving toward others.

Reality Bite

Have students take steps toward radical selflessness. Have them take on one or more of the following aggressive goals:

• Each day next week, do something kind and loving for ten people.

• Invest half your free time next week in loving those who are not your peers.

• Next Saturday spend half the day visiting and cleaning the house of an elderly person in your church.

• Worship the Lord for a half-hour each day next week. When you are thinking of nothing in particular, inject a few thoughts about God and how wonderful he is.

Family Devotion Online!

See www.youthministry.com/family_devos for an activity-packed family devotion that you can download for free and copy for your students' parents.

10. Breaking Free

Topics

Bad habits, drugs and alcohol, sin

Scripture Base

Genesis 6:5-6; Proverbs 15:9; Matthew 5:6, 29-30

The Point

Sinful habits can weaken and destroy us, so they must be dealt with quickly, forcefully, and decisively.

Stuff You'll Need

TV and VCR, the movie *The Sandlot* (20th Century Fox), masking tape

Preparation

Before the session, tape one or more big circles (twelve feet across) on the floor of your room. (Create one circle for every five students, or plan to have groups of five take turns.) Circles should be several feet apart.

Write the Commitment Cores questions on a chalkboard or a sheet of newsprint.

Introduction

Leadership Tip

For most young people who have only dabbled in the world of drugs and other similar sinful habits, this message holds enough to help them break free. Students who are up to their necks in addiction or deep into drugs should be referred to a competent Christian counselor.

Leadership Tip

If you have a large group, consider doing this with four or five small groups while the rest of the group cheers them on.

Busting Loose

Have students form groups of five people. Each group should stand by one of the circles taped on the floor. Have one student from each group stand in the middle of a circle while the other four members in each group stand just outside the circle. The person in the middle will be allowed one minute to try to flee the circle without being touched by the other four students standing outside the circle. If the person in the middle successfully busts loose without being touched (or if one minute is up), another person in that group will take a turn in the middle. Continue until everyone has had a chance to be in the middle and to try to bust loose. Then lead a short discussion.

• What kinds of skills were required to bust loose from your circle? to touch the person trying to bust loose?

• How was being in the middle and trying to bust loose like someone trying to break free from a sinful habit?

You know when people start doing a drug or taking a substance, they typically have no idea what could possibly happen. But others get a good indication right from the start.

The Sandlot

To show a bad first-time experience with substance abuse that illustrates the risks involved, play a clip from The Sandlot. *Begin the clip at 49 minutes, 30 seconds when a kid holds up a bag of chewing tobacco. End the clip at 52 minutes, 30 seconds when the team exits the ride, covered in vomit. Warning: This scene is pretty gross.*

This could actually be a blessing in disguise. Drugs distort perceptions. They mess up the mind, making it harder to hear God. They too easily become something drug users run to when they're anxious, stressed, or experiencing problems. They use them to wimp out and escape their problems or challenges rather than be strong and face them head-on.

Remember, every alcoholic, every junkie, and every chain smoker had to have that first drink, toke, or smoke. And every one of them thought they were too smart, too tough, too good, or too strong to get hooked. Boy, were they ever surprised. Tragically, some of them pay for their mistakes with their lives.

Even if we don't get hooked, drugs have a funny way of becoming part of our lives. Some people can't even have a good time without drugs—they're prisoners. What a trap. Others are so desperate to be cool that they just have to have that cancer stick blazing in their hands. Some have relationships built all around drug use—it's sad.

I've got good news today. If you're a Christian, you have the power within you to overcome every sin and every habit. No matter what it is, you can be free!

Today let's look at how to break free from illicit drug use or any other sinful habit.

The Message

Key Point #1: Recklessly embrace radical righteousness!

Read Matthew 5:6.

What do you think it means to hunger and thirst for righteousness—to crave it like food? *Encourage response.* How do you know when you hunger and thirst for righteousness? *Encourage response.*

To help build thirst and hunger, we need to do a few mind aerobics, saying to ourselves things like "I am all about pleasing God," and asking key questions like "Does what I am doing please God?", "I'm all about helping people and loving people, so will this harm me or others?", "Is it destructive or constructive?", "Does this draw me closer to God?", and "Do I reflect Christ when I do this?"

We can regain our affection for righteousness and righteous desires by committing ourselves to doing right things like service, ministry, missions, helping, reaching out to those in need, and teaching. Right emotions follow right actions.

Truly only God can put a hunger and thirst for righteousness inside us. But I know that as we pattern our decisions, our choices, and our very lives on Christ and the wonderfully loving, gentle, peaceful, yet mighty life he modeled for us, we will begin to understand that thirst and hunger. It springs from our love for him. That love will not allow us to do things that would hurt him in any way.

God is our source of hunger and thirst for righteousness.

Key Point #2: Unleash a sin-hating attitude!

Read Proverbs 15:9 and Genesis 6:5-6.

The Lord detests the way of the wicked. When he saw the sin of man at the time of Noah, God grieved over it "and his heart was filled with pain" (Genesis 6:6).

Sin hurts God, but he hates it most of all because it separates people from him. God hates sin because it destroys people, even kills them. Sin keeps people from God's best plan for their lives. It distracts people from their purpose and from his plans for them.

So we must learn to hate sin. The best way to do this is to remind ourselves what sin does. I'll mention several different sins. As I do, call out the destruction and harm that can befall someone who participates in the sin and the effect it can have on others, like friends, family, Christians, and non-Christians. Drunkenness? *Allow response.* Stealing? *Allow response.* Drug high? *Allow response.* Lying? *Allow response.* Violence and rage? *Allow response.* Sexual addiction or pornography habit? *Allow response.*

Unleash a sin-hating attitude!

Key Point #3: Take immediate, bold action!

Read Matthew 5:29-30.

How many think Jesus is telling us to gouge out our eyes or to cut off our hands if we sin? Wrong-o! Jesus is speaking figuratively here. He is speaking of the absolute importance of having a zero tolerance for sin. Too many of us tolerate sin in our lives, which, if left unchallenged, could eventually destroy us.

It's better to experience the short-term pain of removing sin from our lives than to allow sin to bring judgment and condemnation to our lives.

When confronting sin in our lives, we must be ruthless and bold, showing no mercy. Remember, sin, if left alone, will steal peace and joy from you. It will try to destroy you spiritually, physically, or emotionally. It's a thief stealing from you. It's a spiritual cancer. So rip it out of your life!

Sin-Ripping

Give each person two six-inch strips of masking tape. Have students stick these strips on their right arms, parallel to each other, and smooth them out. At your signal, students should start slowly ripping one masking tape strip off their arms.

• How did that feel?

Now have students quickly remove the other piece of tape from their arms. Then lead a short discussion.

• Which did you prefer: the long, slow burn approach of tearing the tape slowly from your arm or the quick rip? Why?

• How was this like the approaches one can take to break free from drug use or other sinful habits?

• How can removing sin from our lives be painful?

The best approach to quitting any bad habit is to rip it out immediately. We must make a bold decision to get the drug or habit out of our lives, no "just one sip" or "one more time can't hurt!"

Next we must make a rock-solid commitment to stay free from the sin. Then it's vital that we become accountable to a more mature Christian to help us stand firm against the temptation.

We shouldn't put off breaking free from bad habits and sins that stick. If we wait, we may get to the point when—much to our surprise and horror—we're no longer capable of breaking free. Let me tell you a story to illustrate this.

Flying Free

Over the majestic, wintry waterfall, the sun was going down. The snow-outlined, icy falls had a breathtaking beauty. Birds around the falls were flying free, their bold silhouettes set against a multicolored sky.

As I watched the birds, one bird stood out from the rest. He was a wild one, yet expert in his abilities. He soared, he dove, and he darted. He flew where none of the other birds dared to fly. He would soar right into the heavy, icy mist above the falls then shoot back up with amazing speed and agility.

I watched him dive down again, his closest dive to the falls yet. And that's when it happened. As he tried to soar up again, his motions were jerky and erratic, not performed with the amazing grace he had earlier exhibited. He was struggling.

He had stayed so close to the misty falls for so long that his wings were iced and heavy. Lower and lower the grand bird flew until his body disappeared into the torrent and dashed against the rocks at the bottom of the falls.

We must forcefully and aggressively rip from our lives bad habits and sins that stick.

Closing Challenge

If you want to break free from drugs or any other sin that is holding you in bondage, you've got to unleash that sin-hating attitude, hunger, and thirst for righteousness and be willing to do whatever it takes to rip that sin immediately out of your life and never turn back to it again. With God's help there's no habit and no drug that you cannot overcome.

Commitment Cores

Have students form groups of two or three to discuss these questions:

• When have you seen harm come to people who fell into habitual sin or drug abuse? What was the outcome?

• How satisfied are you with your hunger and thirst for righteousness? Why? What are you going to do about it?

• What is one habit or behavior in your life that you most need to get rid of? Why? How do you intend to get rid of it?

• What one thing will you immediately commit to do to break free from that sin or habit—and how can we help you?

Family Devotion Online!

See www.youthministry.com/family_devos for an activity-packed family devotion that you can download for free and copy for your students' parents.

Have students pray for one another in their groups according to what was shared. Then close the session by praying that you and the students would gain a hunger and thirst for righteousness as well as a hatred for sin. Pray that you will all be pleasing to God in all your ways.

Reality Bite

Have a local law enforcement agent talk to the students about the dangers of drug use and provide case studies and true stories of what has happened to drug users to give a necessary, real-life warning of the risks.

11.

One Thing Never Changes—Change

Topics

Changes, life is an adventure

Scripture Base

I Samuel 17:17-30; 18:1-16; 20

The Point

Life is full of changes, so the better we accept and navigate these changes, the better off we'll be.

Stuff You'll Need

TV and VCR, the movie *Father of the Bride* (Touchstone Pictures, 1991), index cards, pens

Preparation

Before the session, you may want to write each of the Rapid-Change Role-Plays (see page 65) on separate index cards.

Write the Commitment Cores questions on a chalkboard or a sheet of newsprint.

Introduction

Let's see how sensitive we are to change.

Eye for Change?

Have group members take a good look around the room, then ask them to leave the room. Move or rearrange items in the room. Have students come back in and try to identify which things were moved. Do at least two or three rounds of this, then lead a short discussion.

• What skills were required to do well in this game?

• As skilled as you were in noticing changes in the room, we all missed a lot of changes as well. How could some of these changes have slipped by you? Explain.

Leadership Tip

If you have more than thirty people in your group, it may be quite time-consuming to get them in and out of the room. Consider playing several rounds, but each time have a small group of five to ten people step out of the room and return.

Some say that the only thing that remains the same in life is change. And we're probably all cool with change when the change holds bigger and better things for us. But when change threatens to take away someone we love or something we enjoy, change becomes difficult to handle. Let's talk about change today.

The Message

Key Point #1: Change surprises!

Father of the Bride

To make a point about how change can be surprising, show a clip from Father of the Bride. *Begin the clip at 9 minutes, 00 seconds when the father says, "Paul Simon's coming to the Forum." End the clip at 11 minutes, 45 seconds when the father says, "Why's it so hot in here?" Then lead a short discussion.*

- What changes are in store for the daughter? for the father?
- How do their reactions to change differ? Why?

The funny thing about change is, you never seem prepared for it, and it leaves you no choice. It just kind of happens.

Summarize I Samuel 17:17-30.

When his kid brother David showed up at the front lines of battle, Eliab didn't see a man who had killed a lion and a bear; he saw only his kid brother. Imagine then his shock, dismay, and embarrassment when David boldly asked the soldiers around them, "Who is this uncircumcised Philistine that he should defy the armies of the living God?" (verse 26).

Eliab burned with anger and accused David of being conceited and wicked. David responded with a characteristic younger-brother-with-older-brother-always-on-my-case attitude: "Now what have I done? Can't I even speak?" (You never let me do anything with you and your friends, Eliab!)

Somewhere, sometime David had grown up, and Eliab still didn't realize it. Some of us know people who never seem to get that we're grown up now—we're not the kids we used to be. By the same token, some of us haven't realized that there are people in our lives who aren't kids anymore either.

We need to be aware that some people, like parents and current friends, will have difficulty keeping up with our changes, so we need to cut them some slack and a little understanding. Be patient, they'll get it. But don't do anything crazy to let them in on it. When parents treat you like a kid or friends try to get you to do the fun things you used to do together, things you now consider to be dumb or immature, gently remind them of who you are now. When you're with your parents, behave like the adult you want them to see. And try to find some new common ground with your friends. Change always seems to surprise us.

Key Point #2: Change separates!

Read or summarize I Samuel 18:1-16.

David had just killed Goliath. Saul immediately took David into his household. Saul's son, Jonathan, became David's closest friend. Suddenly the life of this shepherd boy was changed forever. In one day he went from anonymity to celebrity. He left his family for a new life in the king's household.

But later on, David's life changed dramatically again. Saul became jealous of David because the people respected David and loved him more than Saul. Saul feared David. He even tried to pin David to the wall with a spear—twice. Saul separated himself from David.

Sometimes our changes, or those of our friends or family, threaten to pull our relationships apart. We wonder, "Is it over for us?" It doesn't always have to be that way. It all depends on how you navigate the tension and how well you communicate with the other person. Let's practice navigating some pretty tricky changes.

Rapid-Change Role-Plays

Have students form six groups. Assign each group one of the scenarios below. Each group should role-play a short, but believable, realistic resolution for each scenario. After about three minutes, have groups perform their role-plays. Then lead a short discussion.

• What were some of the most creative resolutions you heard just now? Explain.

• Which of these changes would be most difficult for you to handle? Why?

• What are some important attitudes to have when we face changes like these in people we know?

Rapid-Change Scenarios

1. Your mom and dad are getting a divorce. You're feeling confused and angry. You don't really want to talk about it. Your dad, the one who initiated the divorce, is telling you about all the benefits of the divorce and how things will change, most notably that you'll live with your mom from now on.

2. You don't have time for your friends anymore, now that you have a girlfriend or boyfriend. One of your friends is walking up to confront you about this.

3. Your father's company is transferring him to another state, and you'll be moving away in a few months. You haven't told your friends because you keep hoping it won't happen. One of your friends confronts you because you seem to be pulling away from everybody else.

4. You don't know why, but you just woke up feeling "out of love" with your girlfriend or boyfriend of four months. Lately you've been feeling like the relationship is a bit stale. This is the end. You don't want to hurt the person's feelings, but you have to tell the truth. He or she is walking toward you now.

5. Lately you've been feeling awkward and immature hanging around the mall arcade with friends. You're growing up and out of these things—not playing Nintendo and PlayStation much at all anymore. You're getting into sports and outside stuff. Your friend asks why you're no fun anymore.

6. Your friend (well, she used to be your friend until four months ago) has radically changed in her appearance and in other ways. She used to be quiet, dress conservatively, and listen to bubble gum pop bands. Now she's wearing black, listening to hard music, and hanging with a loud crowd that curses freely and smokes over a pack a day. She also colored her hair bright red. She runs into you in the restroom. You miss her friendship, but she feels she has moved on.

Though changes can threaten to permanently pull us apart from friends and family members, they don't have to.

Keepin' It Real!

Share with students a time in your own life when a change in you or a friend caused a separation between the two of you—even temporarily. Talk about how you handled it and what you learned.

Key Point #3: Change stops and starts relationships.

Summarize I Samuel 18:1-4; 20.

Even though Saul caused the sun to set on his relationship with David, the sun began to rise and continued to rise on David and Jonathan's relationship. Sometimes change does present insurmountable differences in relationships, and people do go their separate ways. But changes can open up new opportunities for friendship as well. Sometimes it can be hard to tell the difference.

Three's a Crowd!

Read the following true story to students.

Last year, one of the worst things in my life happened: My best friend got a boyfriend. I know that shouldn't be such a big deal, but it was for me.

Dana and I had been best friends for about a year and a half. We did everything together…We were inseparable. She had liked this guy named Scott for about as long as we had been friends. When we found out he liked her, too, you can imagine how excited we both were. I was happy for her…

When they started going out, Dana and I still did most things together. If Scott was there, it wasn't a problem. You know the saying "Two's company; three's a crowd"? That didn't apply to our situation at all. During the first two months, Dana was her usual fun, caring, and sensitive self. She was there for me when my grandmother went into the hospital and when my aunt and uncle divorced.

But…three started to become a crowd. I felt like an extra, unwanted and unneeded. Dana stopped calling me as often, and when she did call, all she wanted to talk about was Scott. It seemed as though she didn't want to hear what was going on in my life. I felt hurt and confused, as if I was losing my best friend to a guy.

I didn't tell her what was going on inside my confused head; I tried to act as I normally did when I was around her…I started to back away from her and avoided her whenever possible.

One Sunday at church…she had been teasing me about a guy…and I blew up…I cried so hard…Dana and I left church without speaking to each other…I wrote her a letter that week, explaining everything…We finally talked about it, and after we shed a few more tears, I thought our relationship would return to normal. But even though we called each other, our friendship wasn't the same.

I finally realized that I hadn't forgiven her. I didn't trust her and didn't want to be hurt again. She started ignoring me again, and I became just as confused as the first time…I wrote her another letter and put our relationship in God's hands. Through a lot of conversations and prayer, we finally forgave each other. God gave me peace about what had happened, and we are best friends again. (Excerpted from *Doing Life With God* by Bo Boshers.)

Lead a short discussion.

• Who can identify with what the speaker, Heather, is feeling? Why?

• How would you have handled this situation? Why?

• What can we learn from this story about changes in life?

The best way to handle feelings of separation from friends or family or of fear that a relationship may be over is direct, honest communication—like the letter this girl wrote to her friend to tell her how she felt. Be sure to listen. Overall, we need to assure and remind doubting people that the love we have felt for them is still there. We must let them know we still care deeply for them. Try to be open to a new and different relationship with them. Think about your friend and whether it's in his or her best interest to move on or stay in the relationship.

Finally, be ready to let go of a relationship if the new differences are just too much for you both to overcome. Recall and treasure the good times. Not all friendships are lifelong. Change brings new relationships and ends some old ones.

Closing Challenge

Change is good, but it may present some difficult challenges or even threaten some of our longest-term and most deeply treasured friendships. That's when we need to remember to show every ounce of grace and love we can and to clearly communicate with friends and family members.

Commitment Cores

Have students form groups of two or three to discuss these questions:

• Can best friendships we had when we were kids last a lifetime? Why? How?

• Tell about a treasured relationship you had with someone that ended due to changes in one or both of you.

• What changes are you, a family member, or a close friend undergoing that are affecting your relationships?

• What one thing will you do in your closest relationships to keep changes from causing harm or separation?

Have students pray for one another within their groups according to what was shared. Then close in prayer, asking God to help students be more loving and gracious toward those they love, especially when they undergo change. (Thank God for never changing!)

Reality Bite

Have people from the congregation come to your meeting. Interview them about significant life changes they've undergone and how God was with them during those times. They should also share how these changes affected their relationships with God and with close friends and family members. If people aren't able to come in and share, videotape the interviews beforehand.

Family Devotion Online!

See www.youthministry.com/family_devos for an activity-packed family devotion that you can download for free and copy for your students' parents.

12. God Is Speaking

Topics

God's voice, availability and obedience to God, seeking God

Scripture Base

Deuteronomy 5:32-33; Matthew 13:14-16

The Point

Hearing God is essential to living the incredible life God has planned for us.

Stuff You'll Need

TV and VCR, the movie *Apollo 13* (Universal Pictures), copy of the "Who? What? Where?" handout (p. 72), copies of the "Ways God Speaks" handout (p. 73), copies of the skit "Dirk Hears God" (pp. 74-75)

Preparation

Before the session, recruit five people for the skit "Dirk Hears God" (pp. 74-75). They should practice an hour to be fully prepared for the skit.

Write the Commitment Cores questions on a chalkboard or a sheet of newsprint.

Introduction

Turn to a partner, and tell him or her about a time you or someone you know heard God speak—and what God said. *Allow students a minute or two to do this. Then have students share how easy or difficult it is to hear God.*

Let's see how difficult communication can be.

Who? What? Where?

Have students form five mime troupes. Assign each mime troupe one of the scenarios listed on the "Who? What? Where?" handout (p. 72). Each troupe should create a sixty-second pantomime for the rest of the group. Allow troupes a minute or two to plan what they'll do. Then have each troupe perform its pantomime. The rest of the group should call out what's being pantomimed until they correctly guess who, what, and where.

If the group is stumped, either allow troupes more than a minute to pantomime, or simply let the group know what the troupe was trying to mime. After each group has performed its pantomime, lead a short discussion.

• How easy or difficult was it for you to figure out these pantomimes?

• What skills were required to correctly figure these out?

• How was this like or unlike hearing God?

Too many people believe that hearing God is just as elusive and difficult as playing this game. But A.W. Tozer, a famous Christian writer and pastor, once said, "The blessed fact is that God is not silent and has never been silent, but is speaking in His universe…He desires to communicate Himself, to impart holy ideas to those of His creatures capable of receiving them" (excerpted from *God Tells the Man Who Cares* by A.W. Tozer). We just have to be listening and capable of receiving what God says. Let's find out how God speaks and how to be in a position to hear him today.

The Message

Key Point #1: Why God speaks

Read Deuteronomy 5:32-33.

God speaks because he wants us to enjoy a wonderful, satisfying, joyful, purposeful, adventurous life–with him! He wants us to know him. He wants to express his love to us. Because there are so many lies in our world, he wants us to know the truth. He wants us to have an open line of communication so he can help us navigate even the smallest details of daily life. The only way to enjoy this is by living our lives in obedience to the Lord's voice.

God speaks so we'll know how to live the most incredible life possible.

Key Point #2: How God speaks

Dirk Hears God

Have actors perform the skit "Dirk Hears God" (pp. 74-75), then lead a short discussion.

• What are some ways God spoke to Dirk in this skit?

• What skills are required to hear God in these ways?

There are many ways God speaks to us. *Distribute the "Ways God Speaks" handout (p.73). Read it with the group.*

God Speaking?

Read the following statements to the group. After you read each one, students should stand and say "he-llo!" if they think it presents a way God speaks to us. If they don't think it presents a way God speaks, they should stay seated and shake their heads. Invite students to say why they voted as they did.

• Mom or Dad speaks with you, concerned about your new friend.

• You see a mountain range and are struck by its beauty.

• You see an elderly couple walking along, holding hands.

• Some friends invite you to a party, but you don't feel peace about going.

• You're sharing Christ with a guy, and he brings up a sin he knows you commit and asks, "What makes you different from me?"

• You see a homeless person sitting on the sidewalk.

• You feel God calling you to a mission trip, but you have no money.

Keepin' It **Real!**

Share a time you felt that God spoke to you and how this led you into something that was God's best for you.

Keepin' It **Real!**

Tell students of a time you heard from God in an unusual or humorous way.

• A Christian friend advises you to flee your dating relationship with someone who is pressuring you for sex.

• You begin to weep as an inner-city minister tells you about her ministry.

• You see a beautiful butterfly in flight.

• You sit alone in the woods, admiring the tall trees.

Lead a short discussion.

• What's your reaction to the realization that God could speak to us in all these ways?

• Since God is able to speak in so many different ways, why is it so hard for us to hear him sometimes?

God is constantly speaking to us in one way or another!

Key Point #3: Who God speaks to

Apollo 13

Show a good clip concerning the importance of finding guidance. Begin Apollo 13 at 1 hour, 45 minutes when Jim Lovell is interviewed on television, recounting the time his fighter plane failed. End the clip at 1 hour, 46 minutes, 30 seconds when the interview ends. Then lead a short discussion.

• What saved Jim Lovell from tragedy?

• The pilot in this clip realized that his life depended on staying focused on his instruments and then the wake of the ship. How important is staying focused and dependent on God's voice? Why?

God speaks to and is heard by those who desperately want to hear him.

Read Matthew 13:14-16.

What did Jesus mean by what he said in these verses? *Encourage response.* How do you think people who hear God get to the point where they hear but don't understand? see but never perceive? have a calloused or hardened heart? *Encourage response.* Those who will hear God speak are those who have ears open to listening to him, eyes that look constantly to him, and a heart that treasures the word he speaks. In short, those who are seeking God will find him.

God speaks to those who are seeking him, those who...

• are R.A.W.—Ready, Available, and Willing to obey (Isaiah 6:1-9).

• are willing to admit that God knows what's best for their lives better than they do (John 5:19; 8:19-30, emphasis on 8:26-29).

• believe God is telling the truth and the world is lying (Genesis 12:1-4). For example, a person may know what God says about sexual immorality. God doesn't want people to commit sexual immorality, and those who do are rejecting him (1 Thessalonians 4:3-8). The world says, "Anything goes." Therefore, the Christian who commits sexual immorality shows that he or she believes the world over God in this matter.

God is speaking. To hear him consistently, we must seek him, be ready to obey whatever he says, and have a desire to please him in every way.

Closing Challenge

God is constantly speaking in this world of ours. Let's be sure we're capable of hearing and understanding him.

Commitment Cores

Have students form groups of two or three to discuss these questions:

• What would be the coolest way for God to speak to you?

• How capable are you of hearing and understanding God? Why?

• What's one thing in your life that you most need to hear from God about?

• What one thing will you do to be in a better position to hear God and to hear him concerning your response to the previous question? *Students should help one another brainstorm ideas.*

Have students pray in their groups according to what each person shared. Close by praying that everyone will have ears to hear God and eyes that look constantly to him for wisdom and guidance.

Reality Bite

Challenge motivated students to keep a "God talk" journal over the next week. They should record all the wonderful ways God communicates with them as they listen carefully and expect him to speak. At the end of the week, get together and compare journals.

Family Devotion Online!

See www.youthministry.com/family_devos for an activity-packed family devotion that you can download for free and copy for your students' parents.

Who? What? Where?

Cut along the dotted lines and distribute one assignment to each troupe.

Assignment 1

Instructions: Pantomime this scenario for the rest of the group to guess.

Who? A church choir member

What? Carrying a rose

Where? Walking on water

Assignment 2

Instructions: Pantomime this scenario for the rest of the group to guess.

Who? A small girl

What? Balancing a baseball bat in her hand

Where? On a dirt road

Assignment 3

Instructions: Pantomime this scenario for the rest of the group to guess.

Who? A clown

What? Carving a wooden cross

Where? In a train boxcar

Assignment 4

Instructions: Pantomime this scenario for the rest of the group to guess.

Who? A yodeler

What? Fending off a mouse that is creeping up his leg

Where? On a New York City subway

Assignment 5

Instructions: Pantomime this scenario for the rest of the group to guess.

Who? A woman with no teeth

What? Eating cotton candy

Where? At a gas station

Ways God Speaks

- through the Bible (Psalm 119:105)

- through prayer (Acts 13:2-3)

- through our hearts or consciences (Psalm 37:4; Philippians 2:13)

- through our peace (Colossians 3:15)

- through parents (Ephesians 6:1-2)

- through Christian leaders/teachers/youth pastors (Hebrews 13:7)

- through the counsel of others—sometimes

  non-Christians (Proverbs 12:15; 15:22)

- through a still, small voice (1 Kings 19:11-12)

- through dreams and visions (Acts 10:9-34)

- through prophecy or words of wisdom (practical knowledge that comes only

  through special grace and favor of the Lord) and words of knowledge (special

  insight into God's will) (1 Corinthians 12:7-11)

- through an audible voice (Mark 1:9-11)

Characters

Dirk (A Christian who doesn't recognize the many ways that God speaks), Kid, Elderly Woman, Young Woman, and Rick

Props

A ball, a bag of groceries, binoculars

(Dirk is pacing and praying aloud.)

Dirk: Oh Lord, I just know you have something amazing and huge for me to do today. Speak to me, Lord, I am listening.

(Kid bounces ball from offstage, hitting Dirk on the leg.)

Kid: *(Offstage)* Hey, dude, like, can you throw my ball back?

Dirk: So speak to me, Lord, *speak* to me, *please*, God!

Kid: *(Offstage)* OK, can you *please* throw my ball back?

(Dirk walks past the ball. Kid enters, snatches ball, gives Dirk an angry look, and exits. Elderly Woman enters. She struggles to carry her bag of groceries.)

Dirk: Speak, Lord, your faithful servant listens.

(Dirk walks right into the Elderly Woman.)

Dirk: Oh, I am so sorry. I'm a Christian; I'm trying to hear God. Wow, those groceries look heavy...yup, they look real heavy...

(Elderly Woman looks at him hopefully.)

Dirk: *(Turns away.)* Oh, God, *please* speak to me.

(Elderly Woman shakes her head and struggles away. A Young Woman with binoculars enters, watching the sky.)

Young Woman: Oh man, look at that beautiful sunset! You know what? For the first time in my life I think I believe in God. I believe I can know him. Oh my, how I wish someone could tell me how to know God!

Dirk: *(Stops and turns slowly to the Young Woman. She looks at him expectantly. He looks up at the sky.)* That is a beautiful sunset. *(Stands another second or two, then goes back to pacing.)* Speak to me, Lord. Speak to me.

Young Woman: OK, maybe not. *(Exits.)*

(Dirk's friend Rick enters.)

Rick: Dirk, Dirk, man!

Dirk: Hey, dude!

Rick: Dirk, I don't know you very well, but you seem like someone I can really talk to, man. My life is so screwed up, man. I need a change. I need God's peace like you seem to have, man. I need a new start. I need…

Dirk: Rick, I don't mean to be rude, but I am really trying to hear God here, and I keep getting distracted. I really, really need some peace and quiet. Um, maybe we can talk later?

Rick: *(Shocked)* Um, sure, man, whatever. I'll, I'll, uh, check you out later.

Dirk: All right, my man, later. *(Smiles.)*

(Rick turns and leaves.)

Dirk: *Speak,* Lord. What is your will for me today? Speak to me, Lord, your servant is listening!

Get Your Truth On!

Topics

Honesty, pleasing God, character

Scripture Base

Genesis 25:24-34; 27:1-40; Proverbs 12:13, 21-22

The Point

Honesty is the best policy.

Stuff You'll Need

TV and VCR, the movie *Liar Liar* (Universal Pictures), copies of the skit "Jacob and Esau Improv" (pp. 80-81), paper, pencils, a candy bar

Preparation

Before class, write the Commitment Cores questions on a chalkboard or a sheet of newsprint.

Introduction

Let's start with a little pop quiz today! *Allow time for the groans to subside.*

Mind Game

Distribute paper and pencils, keeping one of each for yourself. Have students number their papers from one to ten down the left margin. Tell them that the person with the highest score at the end will win some "brain food."

Think of a number between one and ten, and write it on your paper next to number one. Then have students guess what number you've written and write it on their papers. After students have guessed, tell them the number you chose. They should score themselves in a column to the right of their guesses. If they guessed the correct number, they score ten points; if they missed the correct number by one or two, they score five points; if they guessed within three or four of the correct number they get zero points; if they missed by more than four, they lose five points. It's very important that students score themselves at the end of each round and tell one another how they did.

Play ten rounds. Don't hesitate to use the same number more than once. After ten rounds, determine a winner by totaling points, then award a candy bar to the person with the most points.

Tear off a little piece of paper, and write either "no" or "yes" to the following questions: Did you cheat during this game? Did you erase a number then write in the correct one after you knew it? Did you pretend you guessed correctly?

Collect the small pieces of paper, tally the answers, and tell students the results.

• How did you feel during this game, especially as it became clear that others had more points than you did?

• In this game, what made it tempting to cheat?

• What kept you from cheating?

• Why is it important to be honest even in matters like this game?

• Is honesty really the best policy? Why?

Leadership Tip

Most likely at least one student will cheat in this activity. In this case ask these additional questions if someone does admit to cheating: Why do you think some of us cheated? How is cheating—even in a game like this—a big deal?

Too many people fail to understand that it really matters if we're honest in all things. Some think it's OK to play fast and loose with the truth as long as nobody seems to get hurt. Others value honesty and realize dishonesty always hurts someone. Why be honest?

The Message

Key Point #1: Honesty pleases God!

Read Proverbs 12:22.

God couldn't be clearer. He detests lying and delights in those who are truthful. Why does honesty make God so happy? *Encourage student responses.*

Every temptation to lie contains the inherent question "Do I trust God or myself to handle this situation?" By lying we basically say, "I'm calling the shots in my life—and the best way to handle this situation is to lie."

Our honesty pleases God; he delights in us when we're truthful. Besides, we look more like him when we're honest!

Key Point #2: Dishonesty tears relationships apart.

Dishonesty tears relationships apart while honesty builds relationships. Let's look at how deception tore apart the relationship between two brothers.

Jacob and Esau Improv

Find volunteers to play the roles of Jacob, Esau, Isaac, and Rebekah in this narrated skit on pages 80-81. Distribute scripts. Read the narration as students act out what you say. (Feel free to repeat a line or action if an actor doesn't ham it up sufficiently—have fun!) To involve all students, have them take turns playing the four roles, or have them provide sound effects, play animal roles, or make animal noises. Be very enthusiastic as you read. After the skit, lead a short discussion.

• How do you think God felt about all this deception? about Esau's choice and attitude?

• Why did Jacob do what he did? Esau? Rebekah? Isaac?

• How did dishonesty hurt Jacob? Esau? Rebekah? Isaac?

• To be more pleasing to God, what could Jacob have done? Esau? Rebekah?

• How would honesty have made this a better situation for all involved?

• Why should honesty be important to us?

If Jacob had been honest with his brother and if his mother, Rebekah, had acted a little more mature, a serious family rift that lasted for years could have been avoided. How might the relationship between Jacob and Esau have grown if this had never happened? Dishonesty tears relationships apart!

Key Point #3: Honesty simplifies our lives.

Read Proverbs 12:13, 21.

Sir Walter Scott had it right: "What a tangled web we weave, when first we practice to deceive." And most people probably would say they agree with Sir Walter Scott. But this is the kicker—most people lie because they fool themselves into believing that things will be simpler and easier if they lie. Converting to honesty after being so dependent on dishonesty can be quite an experience.

Liar Liar

To illustrate what an experience it can be for some people to commit to honesty, show a clip from Liar Liar. Tell students the following scenario before playing the clip. Fletcher's son, tired of his father's broken promises to spend time with him, makes a wish that for one day his dad, a lawyer, will not be able to lie. It works!

Begin the clip at 27 minutes, 0 seconds when Fletcher leaves an elevator. End the clip at 29 minutes, 22 seconds when Fletcher gets up from behind his desk and says maniacally, "The pen is blue."

Lying complicates our lives. If you lie, then lie again to cover up the last one, you've got to keep track of all the lies and what you told who. It gets way too complex.

Things get tricky. Maybe not at the moment and maybe not for weeks, perhaps years, but eventually our dishonesty finds us out in one way or another. We feel a strange distance from God or find it hard to look some people in the eyes. Or someone discovers we lied to them. Other times we just feel rotten.

There's nothing like the look in someone's eyes when a friend has lied to him or her. You may say, "Well all my friends are liars—I mean they lie way worse than me, so they understand if they catch me in a lie." No, they won't. As a Christian you just might be their one gleaming beacon of hope that somebody out there in this lie-filled world had the guts to tell the truth.

Trust me. Telling the truth will make your life a lot easier.

Keepin' It Real!

OK, we opened the can of worms. Share about a time you lied to a friend and the consequences of that.

Closing Challenge

Mark Twain said, "When in doubt, tell the truth. It will confound your enemies and astound your friends." I believe we've heard a few better reasons today than confounding and astounding other people. But it does get back to the point that in one way or another dishonesty always hurts somebody.

Lying Doesn't Pay

A woman was arrested after forging her $20 lottery ticket, hoping to cash in on a winning number. She didn't know that her lottery ticket, a real winner, would have earned her $2 million without her forgery. Instead of becoming a millionaire, she went to jail, which is just another example of how lying doesn't pay—literally.

Lead a short discussion.

• What point did you get out of this story?

• What does this story tell you about the importance of honesty?

Let's please the Lord by being people of honesty and integrity.

Commitment Cores

Have students form groups of two or three to discuss these questions:

• Tell of a time you were hurt by someone else's lie.

• To most people you know, is lying a sin or a strategy? Why?

• How would a commitment to total honesty change your life?

• What one thing will you do to be more honest?

Have students pray for one another in their groups according to what they shared. Close the session by praying that you and every student will please God in all your ways, particularly in honesty, integrity, and strength of character.

Reality Bite

Have motivated students set out to be absolutely honest in every way over the next week. They should keep a record of all their deceptions or untruths for an entire week. They can do this by carrying around a card and tallying each incident. Incidents can be anything from misrepresenting attitudes and opinions to little white lies and outright lies. It's important to keep this activity light. It must not come off as harsh. It's simply an experiment.

At week's end, get together with the students and ask them to share, in general, how it went and any surprises they experienced.

Extra Idea and Family Devotion Online!

See www.youthministry.com/family_devos for one more idea to illustrate Key Point #3 and an activity-packed family devotion that you can download for free and copy for your students' parents.

Jacob and Esau Improv

(Loosely based on Genesis 25:24-34; 27:1-40)

Instructions: Read the following narration as group members act it out.

Actions for characters are in **bold**. Sound effects, animal roles, and crowd parts are in parentheses to be performed by everyone not playing one of the four key roles.

Scene 1

From the time they were born to Rebekah and Isaac, Esau and Jacob competed with each other. **("Awww, aren't they cute?") (As everyone cheered for them)**, Esau and Jacob **arm wrestled...they threw each other around...they thumb wrestled.** Even when they were born, Jacob had a hold of his brother's ankle! It sounds like Esau was a man's man who liked to **strike a certain bodybuilder pose ("ooh-aah")...and another one ("ooh-aah")...and another one ("ooh-aah").** He was an outdoorsy type and a skillful hunter. When he was hunting, he **watched (the deer milling about)** and loved nothing better than **catching one and hogtying it ("yee-haw!").** Jacob was a quiet man who liked to **veg out at home.**

As the boys grew, it became obvious that Isaac favored Esau over Jacob because he **called out to Esau, "Hey, Tiger!" and "Hey, Sport!" and hugged him in a way that made it look like they were sumo wrestling ("awww").** While Isaac would say to Jacob, **"Hey, you, what's your name?"** But Rebekah favored Jacob. She would call out to Jacob, **"Hey, Jacob, the son I like most, my little schnoogums!"** and **kiss him in front of his friends (who made loud kissing noises while she did this).**

Now once Jacob was home **slurping some stew** when he heard Esau come **staggering in, falling and (sounding like a herd of buffaloes).** Esau was coming in from the field, **huffing and puffing, doing push-ups and somersaults.** He was hungry! He said to Jacob gruffly, **"Quick, give me some of that soup! I'm hungry over here!"** Jacob said, **"No soup for you!"** Esau **got down on his knees and begged in a whiny voice, "Please, oh pretty please, give me some of that soup. I'm dying here!"** Jacob thought for a minute then said, **"First sell me your birthright!"**

Esau said, **"Look, I'm dying here and you're wanting my lousy birthright?"** Jacob said, **"Promise me and the soup is yours."** So Esau **gave Jacob a fancy handshake and then swore an oath to him,** selling his birthright to Jacob. **("Cha-ching!")** So Jacob **gave him some bread and lentil stew.** Esau despised his birthright.

Scene 2

Isaac was getting up in years, and his eyes were weak. He called to Esau, **"Hey, Sport, come over here!"** because Isaac thought he would die soon. He wanted to bless Esau before he died. So he **sent Esau out into the field to hunt wild game and fix a meal for him.** So Esau **jumped on one of the donkeys that (brayed loudly).** The donkey **(carried him to a good hunting spot and brayed some more).**

Rebekah overheard Isaac speaking to Esau, and she immediately got an idea **("ding!")** for how to get Jacob the blessing. **Rebekah sent Jacob out to catch two goats. Jacob captured and carried the goats ("baaad news! Baaaad news!")** to Rebekah, who **cooked them up as a meal** for Isaac.

Rebekah **put Esau's best clothes on Jacob and covered his smooth nonhairy skin with goat skins. She handed him the food to give his father and pushed him into his father's room. Then she spit in her hands and smoothed his hair down on top. ("Eewww!")**

Jacob **said in as deep a voice as he could possibly say it, "My father?"**

"Hey, Sport!" Isaac answered, **"Who is it?"**

Jacob responded, **"I'm Ja—uh—Esau, your firstborn. I've got some of your favorite food here!"**

"Come close so I can touch you to know if you're really Esau." Jacob **moved closer to his father,** Isaac, who **touched his face and his arm muscles, mussed his hair, and gave him a noogie. "Good to have you here, Sport!"** Isaac said. Isaac **kissed him and blessed him** and promised him prosperity, that the nations would serve him, and lots of other great stuff.

Jacob had barely left his father's presence when Esau **came riding in on his donkey, which (brayed loudly).** Esau **stumbled and fell as he hurried to prepare the meal for his father and then presented it to him.** Isaac was furious when he realized that Jacob had stolen Esau's blessing.

Esau **burst out with a loud and bitter cry, "Waaah! Waaah!"** And his dad **lost it and yelled, "Waaah! Waaah! Let's call a waaambulance!"** Esau **pleaded on his knees, "Please, father, just one blessing!"** But instead he received a warning that he would dwell away from prosperity and that he would live by the sword and serve his brother. Esau held such a grudge against Jacob that he planned to kill him after his father died.

Fly Like an Eagle!

Topics

Expectations (high and low), pleasing others, purpose

Scripture Base

Esther; Matthew 14:25-33; Mark 6:34-44

The Point

We were made to grow from high expectations, but expectations that are too high or too low can be harmful.

Stuff You'll Need

TV and VCR, copies of the skit "Got Expectations?" (pp. 88-89), the movie *Parenthood* (Universal Pictures), tables, fifteen plastic cups (any size) for every five students, masking tape, upbeat music, CD player

Preparation

Several days before the session, find two people to perform the skit "Got Expectations?" They should practice an hour or so to do well.

Before the session, set up tables on one side of your room. Write the Commitment Cores questions on a chalkboard or a sheet of newsprint.

Introduction

Leadership Tip

If you have fifty or more people in your group, have ten people come forward and compete in two teams, and revise the discussion accordingly.

Championship Cup-Stacking

Have students form teams of five people each. Give each team fifteen cups. Have teams place their cups on the table then form lines at the opposite end of the room. To play the game, one person from each team will race to the table, create a five-tier pyramid from the cups, disassemble the same pyramid, and run back to the team. Each team member should do the same. Teams have one minute and forty seconds (twenty seconds per player) to do this. Play upbeat music to start the game. Turn it off when time is up. As students play, encourage them to go faster and faster and to shave off more and more seconds. Play three more rounds of this, shortening total playing time by at least twenty seconds each time. Then lead a short discussion.

- What one word best describes how you felt during this game?
- What did you think of my expectations of you?
- How did people respond as my expectations increased? Why?

Expectations, you gotta love them. Let's look more closely at them today—and the problem with a lack of them.

Got Expectations? Scene 1

Have actors perform Scene 1 of "Got Expectations?" (p. 88).

• What are your initial observations of Dave and Dwayne?

The Message

Key Point #1: Soar with the eagles!

Summarize Mark 6:34-44.

I'd say Jesus' challenge to the disciples was a little bit tough. He basically said, "Go feed five thousand people with no food and no money!" without saying right off that he would help in any way. That's a high expectation. Jesus did the miracle, but he allowed the disciples to participate. What do you think Jesus was trying to teach? *Encourage students to respond.* One thing they could have learned was that no matter what task was laid before them, with God nothing is impossible.

In what way are high expectations good? *Encourage student responses. Then make any of the following points that students don't make.*

• **They stretch us.** They show us we're smarter, stronger, braver, and better than we thought we were.

• **They move us beyond our comfort zones.** They push us out of that rut, out of that been-there-done-that trap so we can be surprised again.

• **They build faith.** Your impossibility is God's opportunity. Big expectations can help you see, "God did this because there's no way I could have."

• **They build self-confidence and self-image.** When you're pushed beyond your max, you'll be amazed at what new abilities, talents, skills, and qualities rise to the surface.

• **They bring *big* victories.** Big challenges bring big victories.

• **They bring growth and learning.** Whether you win or lose, succeed or fail, you'll learn a lot from big challenges.

• **They help us find our destinies.** The preacher must preach a first time to begin to realize the gift. The runner must run that first lap to discover the passion. Do a bunch of things for God—and you'll discover his purpose for you.

Higher and Higher Hurdles

Have two people stand eight feet apart, each holding one end of the masking tape as a hurdle. They should begin the game holding the "hurdle" about six inches off the floor. As your upbeat music plays, have the rest of the students jump the hurdle. Set the hurdle to one foot, then one and a half feet, having students jump the hurdle each time. Those holding the tape should be instructed to move with the people who run into the tape so they don't trip them.

How many of you are confident now that you can go a little bit higher? *Have only those who respond positively jump from now on. Set the hurdle to two feet. Have students jump. Then lead a short discussion.*

• How many of you knew you could jump like you did in this game?

Leadership Tip

If any of your students are limited in physical ability, have just five or six students jump, and make it a demonstration rather than an activity for the group.

- Why do you think you quit or kept trying as the hurdle was raised?
- What did you learn about expectations from this? about yourself?

Sometimes parents, teachers, youth pastors, or others ask us to do big things—sometimes beyond what we think we can do. These are the times we must at least give God a chance to help us meet those high expectations. Our impossibility is God's opportunity. Let's live to soar with the eagles!

Whatever you do, don't be a chicken like these guys.

Got Expectations? Scene 2

Have actors perform Scene 2 of "Got Expectations?" (p. 88).

- Any additional observations of Dave and Dwayne?
- What impact might low expectations have on us?

Key Point #2: Rise above chickenhood!

Read or summarize Matthew 14:25-33.

You know everybody teaches this story and says, "Look at poor Peter. He just didn't have enough faith, and he fell in. What we can learn from this is that we need a lot of faith." True, but at least Peter got out of the boat!

Sure, Peter fell in when he took his eyes off Jesus and became afraid—but he walked on water! Eleven other guys stayed safe and sound in the boat! Be the one who gets out of the boat and takes risks for God. Be the one who recklessly follows God when others have to sit there and think it through their whole lives. Will you fail at times? You bet! But at least you'll have really lived.

So let's think about the eleven guys who stayed in the boat that night. What's the problem with low expectations? What if we or the adults in our lives really don't expect much of anything from us?

- **We won't be stretched.** We'll do only what we've done before.
- **We'll live snugly inside our comfort zones.** We'll be been-there-done-that people who are safe, secure, and no longer surprised (everything's b-o-o-o-ring).
- **We'll stagnate in faith.** We'll stay quiet, still, and young spiritually.
- **We'll sacrifice self-confidence and self-image.** We'll never discover all that we could have been.
- **We'll see no *big* victories.** Small challenges bring small victories.
- **We won't see growth or learn much more.** No risk equals no growth.
- **We may miss our destinies.** We may miss out on God's best for us.

How Low Can You Go?

Have two people hold the masking tape six inches off the floor. Have all other students jump over the hurdle three times at the same low height. Then lead a short discussion.

- How was it to jump this low hurdle after the hurdles we've jumped?
- What did you learn about expectations from this? What did you learn about yourself?

Keepin' It Real!

Share with students a time you had to overcome some low or negative expectations, how you did it, and the result.

If we aim for low expectations in our lives, we'll hit them every time, but we'll miss out on all the weird and wonderful things we're supposed to accomplish in this life. Be like Peter—get out of the boat. Rise above chickenhood. You're an eagle!

Key Point #3: You were born an eagle!

Summarize the book of Esther, emphasizing Esther becoming queen, Haman's plot to destroy the Jews, Mordecai's challenge to Esther to bring the matter before the king (which would put her life at risk), Esther's plea, and the king's favorable response. Heavily emphasize verse 4:14.

Do you think Esther was born for that moment—to risk her life by speaking up and trying to save an entire nation of people? What moment do you think you might have been born for? All of us are born for a purpose.

Got Expectations? Scene 3

Have actors perform Scene 3 of "Got Expectations?" (p. 89).

• What can we learn from these two guys?

All of us were born to live out a specific life calling and purpose. Let's hear a story about this.

Fly Like an Eagle

Tell students the following story.

A nature lover was once walking through the countryside when he came upon a farm. He walked up to the fence and looked into the barnyard. He saw lots of chickens and geese and other farm animals wandering and scratching about. Then he noticed one bird that didn't fit. He looked more closely and, oddly enough, saw that it was a young eagle, the king of all birds.

So the nature lover climbed the fence, walked into the barnyard, found the farmer, and said, "Sir, I am a nature lover. Do you realize what kind of bird you have here?"

The farmer answered, "Why, yes I do. That's an eagle."

The nature lover replied, "But...but why is this eagle, the king of all birds, scratching around on the ground with chickens, eating and acting like a chicken? Why?"

The farmer said, "When this bird was very young, its mother abandoned it. It grew up in the barnyard, and I just treated it like a chicken. That eagle thinks it's a chicken."

"Well, that's terrible!" the nature lover said. "This is an eagle, the king of all birds. It should be soaring, not groveling about on the ground with these chickens! Do you mind, sir, if I take this young eagle and try to convince him of his destiny?"

"Sure," said the farmer." I don't care what you do with him. He doesn't lay eggs, so he's not helping me any here."

So the nature lover grabbed the young eagle, walked into the center of the barnyard, held him up against the sky, and said to the bird, "You are an eagle, the king of all birds. Stretch forth your wings and fly!" And at that moment, he threw the young bird up into the sky. The bird went up...then he came back down and immediately started flopping and fluttering around on the ground, eating and acting like a chicken.

The farmer, who was watching, said, "I told you! That eagle thinks he's a chicken!"

The nature lover, undaunted, asked permission to take the young eagle up to the top of the barn. "OK," said the farmer. "Do what you want."

So up to the top of the barn the nature lover climbed with the confused bird under his arm. Once they had reached the very rooftop, the nature lover held up the bird against the wind and said again, "You are an eagle, the king of all birds. Stretch forth your wings and fly!"

With that he threw the young bird up into the sky. The bird flopped and fluttered and landed in the barnyard and began eating and acting like a chicken.

The farmer grinned and said, "I told you! He thinks he's a chicken!"

Undaunted, the nature lover grabbed the young eagle, strode out of the barnyard, walked across a field, and climbed a hill. He climbed to the very top of the tallest peak. There, he stood atop a boulder, holding the young bird against the wind, and said once more, "You...you are an eagle, the king of all birds. Stretch forth your wings and fly!"

With that he threw the young bird into the sky. The young eagle stretched forth his wings once...twice...and suddenly, he was flying! He was flying in the autumn sky, becoming all God had created him to be. (Excerpted from *5-Star Stories* compiled by Mikal Keefer.)

- How are we meant to be eagles?
- What are some ways we can, if we're not careful, live like chickens?

The two greatest days of our lives are the day we are born and the day we realize why we were born. All we are experiencing right now, good or bad, is preparing us to live out our ultimate purpose in life. Fly like the eagle you are!

Closing Challenge

Parenthood

To show a case of too high expectations, play a clip from Parenthood. *Begin the video at 12 minutes, 45 seconds when Helen calls her sister. End the clip at 14 minutes, 00 seconds when Patty, the little girl, agrees to try harder.*

Now there are times when expectations are too high. For example, some people set unbelievably high expectations for themselves then tell themselves they're losers or failures when they don't meet them.

Others think God is some grumpy big man in the sky ready to zap them if they don't "perform" and become perfect or become Billy Graham. God just wants us to love him with everything we've got and to love others as ourselves.

Others shrink back from their parents' high expectations—real or imagined. For example, a student may feel like "No way can I tell my parents I'm pregnant!" or "No way can I tell my parents I'm failing high school because I have a drug habit" because "they would be devastated" and "would kill me." They do crazy things to get around telling their parents. They're lying to themselves.

Other teenagers have parents who push them mercilessly in athletics, academics, singing, or acting. If you're dealing with this, you've got to have the big talk with Mom or Dad to ask them to give it a rest. No matter who it is, be honest. Tell them their expectations are way too high, and tell them how you feel like a loser, like you can never please them—whatever you feel.

Don't let anyone talk you out of being who you were meant to be. Don't let anyone keep you from living out the life you were meant to live. God has big plans for you!

Commitment Cores

Have students form groups of two or three to discuss these questions:

• What high expectation do you need help to meet?

• What low expectation do you need to replace?

• What "eagle" purpose do you think God likely has for you? Why?

• What "chicken" things do you need to get out of your life in order to achieve what God has for you? Friends? Habits? Low expectations?

Reality Bite

Together with your group, create a mission statement for your youth ministry—the ultimate goal and thrust of it. Then ask students to think of one thing each of them can do to help the group fulfill that mission over the next month. Then have students follow through on their parts. After a month, note how your youth ministry has changed due to your expectations.

Family Devotion Online!

See www.youthministry.com/family_devos for an activity-packed family devotion that you can download for free and copy for your students' parents.

Got Expectations?

Characters

Dave: An aimless, lazy young guy, wearing the latest and speaking slowly
Dwayne: Same as Dave

Setting and Props

Set up a basement living-room scene. The sofa should face the TV. There should be a coffee table with food containers and empty cola cans all over it. The TV should be placed just right or left of center facing the sofa.

Scene 1

(Dwayne should be sitting on the sofa, mouth open, staring glassy-eyed at the TV. Dave comes and joins him. They should do this for one solid minute. They should take turns sitting up a little bit, as if to talk, but then saying nothing. Finally they speak, slowly and lazily.)

Dave: Dwayne? *(Waits a few seconds.)*

Dwayne: *(Hesitates.)* Yeah?

Dave: What you watching?

Dwayne: I don't know.

Dave: Really? *(Waits.)* You have the remote?

Dwayne: Nope, I guess I lost it…Oh, I think I feel it under me.

Dave: Wow, that's too bad.

(Dave and Dwayne sit silently for another ten or fifteen seconds.)

Scene 2

(Dave and Dwayne are both reclining on the sofa. They sit silently for about twenty seconds.)

Dave: Hey, I think I know what we can do, like, with our lives.

Dwayne: All right!

Dave: You know that crazy guy on TV who catches crocodiles with his bare hands?

Dwayne: Yup.

Dave: Well, I think we could, like, go there, like to Australia, and drive his trucks and stuff for him.

Dwayne: That's cool.

Dave: Yeah.

Dwayne: But don't you, like, have to have a license or something?

Dave: Yeah…you even have to take a test.

Dwayne: Ouch.

Dave: *(Disappointed)* Yeah…what a bummer.

Dwayne: Yeah, a bummer.

(Both guys sit for about ten seconds.)

Scene 3

(Dave and Dwayne are sitting up on the sofa. They sit for about twenty seconds before speaking.)

Dave: Sammy got a job delivering pizza.

Dwayne: Wow, the mother lode!

Dave: Yeah…he said they were hiring.

Dwayne: Ooh yeah…

Dave: So we gonna do it?

Dwayne: Do what?

Dave: Get a job delivering pizzas, man.

Dwayne: *(Pauses for about ten seconds.)* Doesn't pizza delivery require, like, good math skills?

Dave: Ooh, math skills.

(Both guys sit for about ten seconds.)

Dwayne: So's anything good on?

Dave: I dunno.

Dwayne: I hope the crocodile guy comes on soon.

Dave: Yeah…that'd be great.

Dwayne: I wonder if he'll catch something today.

Dave: I sure hope so.

(The guys sit for about ten seconds.)

15. Mind Control

Topics

Evaluating media, renewing the mind, creating standards

Scripture Base

Proverbs 10:23; Romans 12:1-2; 1 Corinthians 6:12; 10:23, 31; 11:1; Philippians 4:8

The Point

Media are made to affect us, so we must be sure they entertain us but don't train us in godlessness.

Stuff You'll Need

TV and VCR, the movie *Wayne's World* (Paramount Pictures), masking tape, poster board, markers

Preparation

Before the session, create a poster for each of the following statements.

A. Don't watch or experience any of it.

B. Watch it and experience it all—it's no big deal. (I mean, come on! Enough already with this "Don't do this, and you can't do that" stuff!)

C. I think it's important to be careful what you listen to and watch—but I actually don't think about it, and I'm not careful what I listen to or watch.

D. Set standards for enjoying media based on what you know pleases God (according to the Bible's and others' standards), and don't violate those standards.

Display the posters in the corners of the room.

Write the Commitment Cores questions on a chalkboard or a sheet of newsprint.

Introduction

Wayne's World

To give students a dose of media influence, show them a clip from Wayne's World. Begin the clip at 48 minutes, 00 seconds when Benjamin approaches Wayne and Garth. End the clip at 49 minutes, 15 seconds when Benjamin leaves Wayne and Garth alone.

Hang on; I think we just suffered some mind control, some media influence! I can control your mind. Want me to prove it? OK.

What *Do* You Do at a Green Light?

Tell students to immediately repeat each word you say or immediately answer any question you ask. As a warm-up have everyone respond immediately to what you say: Too (wait for response), moo (response), boog-a-loo (response). What does a ghost say? (Response.) Make sure students answer immediately.

Now do the actual activity. After you say each word or ask each question, wait for an immediate response: Top, bop, lop. What do you use to clean a floor? *(Mop.)* Crop, sop, hop. Who enforces the law? *(Cop.)* Pop, yop, bop, top. What do you do at a green light? *(Most, if not all, will say "stop.")* Then lead a short discussion.

- How many of you were surprised I could "control your mind" so easily? Explain.

Some people insist that music, movies, magazines, and television have no influence on them. Some students just roll their eyes when they hear adults talk about the negative influence of certain musical artists, movies, and video games. They think, "Not me, this stuff doesn't influence me. I make my own decisions and choices." That response feels right, for sure. But what they fail to understand is that media *exist* to influence them. Multiplied billions of dollars spent each year on advertising through media proves this fact.

Songs can make you feel sad, happy, or strong and fierce. Sometimes they make you think deeply. Movies make you laugh, cry, or respond in a number of ways. So let's look at how to make sure the media we allow to entertain us don't train us or de-brain us.

The Message

Key Point #1: Free your mind...to God!

Four Corners!

Christians typically divide into four camps concerning media. Move to a corner of the room, and stand next to the poster that most closely represents your opinion regarding popular media. Or move to the center if none fits your opinion.

Still standing in their corners (or in the center of the room), have students from each position share their views and why they hold those views. After people have shared their opinions, lead a short discussion.

- Are your standards higher or lower than most people's? than most Christians'? Why?
- How do your standards compare with Jesus' standards?

Read 1 Corinthians 6:12; 10:23, 31; 11:1.

First off, I'm not going to tell you that music, movies, and television shows are the root of all evil and should be avoided at all cost. The issue is not that simple. Though God grants us great freedom to choose in media matters, we must handle this freedom responsibly. He gave us a few guidelines for our freed-up minds and a few more we'll add later.

Everything is permissible...

...but is it beneficial and constructive? Are your media choices beneficial and constructive to you and others? Do they tear down or destroy?

...but does it master you? God loves it when we have fun. But when we're ruled by the quest for the next thrill—pleasure to the exclusion of purpose—even fun can become bad for us.

Are you calling the shots on your choices, or are you just accepting and enjoying anything coming out of the music and movie studios?

...but does it glorify God? God doesn't tell you which songs to like and which movies to watch (or avoid). But his principles and standards are clear in Scripture. Does what you watch, listen to, or do glorify God?

As Christians we must recognize that we cannot make choices only to please ourselves. We should make decisions that please God. We must free our minds...to God!

Key Point #2: Lose your mind...to God!

Read Romans 12:1-2.

Lose your mind! Just be sure to lose it to God, not to media or any godless notions. This passage tells us to offer our bodies (including our hearts and our brains) to God as living sacrifices. We need new brains, not conformed to the pattern of this world but transformed by the renewing of our minds. So go ahead; lose your mind! Just make sure it ends up with God.

As Christians God owns us. Our minds truly belong to him, but many of us don't see it that way. We think they belong to us. We think we can do what we want with them and expose them to just about anything.

Our minds and our will in media choices must be sacrificed to God. God must be allowed veto power over any media choices we make. He owns the right to deny or allow us to experience or not experience every movie, video, song, magazine, or TV show. Submit anything questionable to your parents for their opinion, or seek the help of a mature Christian. Pray to God. Seek these sources for good stuff that will fill and renew your mind.

In this way you lose your mind to God by sacrificing it to him.

Key Point #3: Defend your mind!

Read Proverbs 10:23 and Philippians 4:8.

We can't let just anything into these wonderful minds God has given us. Proverbs tells us we're to delight in wisdom, not to be like a fool who finds pleasure in evil conduct. How does this apply to our media choices? *Encourage responses.* Why do you think it's so important that we do what Philippians 4:8 says and dwell on what is right and good? *Encourage responses.*

Here are some good filters to use when considering media to consume:

M = Message and Means

• **What is the message?** Justice? Love? Violence? Depression?

• **What is the means?** How is the message conveyed? Does the good guy win but only after maiming and torturing the bad guy?

E = Effect

• **What is the effect on me?** Am I moved to compassion? left depressed with no hope?

D = Damage

• **Will I suffer any damage?** Will I have unhealthy fantasies? Will it influence me to pessimism?

I = Instead

• **What could I be doing instead of this?** Could I be doing any constructive, productive, unselfish things rather than vegging and just doing stuff for myself?

Keepin' It Real!

Tell students of a time in your life when you sensed some form of media was not the best influence on you, so you made a change or became choosier in some way.

A = Appeal and Ask God

• **What does this appeal to in me?** Does it build my faith or drive me to righteousness? Does it feed my desire for vengeance? Does it encourage me to lust?

Would I be totally OK with Jesus being here and doing this with me? Would he be entertained by what is entertaining me? Defend your mind!

Keepin' It Real!

Tell students some of your criteria when selecting media to consume.

Closing Challenge

We must practice mind control over media.

A Tragic Death

Tell students the following true story.

On Thursday, May 4, 2000, seventeen-year-old Greg Barnes, star shooting guard for the Columbine High School basketball team, was found dead in his garage. His death came just a few weeks after the one-year anniversary of the deadly shooting at Columbine that shocked the nation.

No one knows why Greg Barnes took his life that Thursday morning. There was no crisis known in his life—no breakup with a girlfriend, no argument with a friend. His conversations and behavior were the same as always the day before his life ended—it just didn't make sense.

Greg was well-liked and popular. He worked hard in class and on the court and excelled in both. He had been voted to the All-Colorado team as one of the top five basketball players in the state. He had received so many invitations and interest letters from colleges and universities that they filled three notebooks. By all accounts, he was a happy and well-adjusted young man.

Barnes had been deeply troubled by the attack on Columbine. "But he didn't dwell on it," according to one friend. "He would talk about it. He was OK with it" (excerpted from RockyMountainNews.com, May 5, 2000).

There was only one clue: The song that was playing repeatedly on the CD player in the garage where his parents found him dead, hanging from an electrical cord. The song set for continuous repeat was "Adam's Song" by the group Blink 182. The lyrics of the song include the phrases "I never thought I'd die alone" and "I'm too depressed to go on. You'll be sorry when I'm gone" (excerpted from DenverPost.com, May 6, 2000).

Lead a short discussion.

• Do you believe music had anything to do with this young man's suicide? Explain.

• What can we learn from this sad death?

It would be naive to say that the Blink 182 lyrics led this young man to his death. But for some reason, Greg was influenced by these lyrics in a way we will never understand—influenced enough for them to become a soundtrack for his death.

Beware of the ability of media—movies, television, music, magazines, and so on—to work as a flash point or cheerleader, fanning your negative emotions into flames. For example, say you're mad at your parents. You may go tearing down the road with loud, angry music blaring out as your anger feeds on raw energy. You may be depressed and play sad or complaint-rock songs all day long, just feeding and cheering on your sadness. Music and media will affect us, but we can and must control our minds and guard ourselves against these effects. We must practice mind control over media.

Commitment Cores

Have students form groups of two or three to discuss these questions:

• What's the worst movie you've ever seen? worst song you've ever heard? Why do they qualify as the worst?

• How do you think media—movies, television, music, magazines, and so on—most influence you? Why?

• What one thing do you most need to change about your media choices?

• What one thing will you do to be more careful in your media choices?

Reality Bite

Challenge students to apply the M.E.D.I.A. method this week and evaluate movies, songs, magazines, and television shows. At the end of the week, have them compare notes, observations, and anything they learned.

As another option, for one week, have students give up one hour a day they would normally spend watching TV, watching movies, or listening to songs. Have them use this time to serve, minister to, or show kindness to others, exchanging a little passive selfish pleasure for unselfish, purposeful action. At the end of the week, talk about how this change affected their lives.

Extra Activity and Family Devotion Online!

See www.youthministry.com/family_devos for an extra activity to add to this message and an activity-packed family devotion that you can download for free and copy for your students' parents.

16. Have G.U.T.S.! (Get off Your Buts!)

Topics

Spiritual courage, moving beyond excuses and perceived limitations

Scripture Base

Exodus 3:1–4:17; 5:1-5; 7:14–11:9; 12:1-42; Numbers 13:1–14:40; 1 Samuel 17; Matthew 3:1-11; Mark 6:17-29; Luke 1:11-17

The Point

To get the most out of our walk with God, we must boldly and bravely give him 100 percent commitment.

Stuff You'll Need

TV and VCR, the movies *Indiana Jones and the Last Crusade* (Paramount Pictures) and *The Sandlot* (20th Century Fox), copies of the skit "God, Incorporated" (pp. 101-102), items chopped in half that must be whole to be used according to their original purposes (such as half a CD or record album, half a car key, half a racquetball, and half a cup), several rolls of pennies

Preparation

Several days before the session, find two volunteers to act out the skit "God, Incorporated." Have them practice at least an hour to prepare before they perform the skit for the group.

Before the session, write the Commitment Cores questions on a chalkboard or a sheet of newsprint.

Introduction

Turn to a partner and tell the person who you think the gutsiest person in the world is and the gutsiest thing you've ever done. *Allow students a moment to share. Have volunteers share their responses with the whole group.*

Probably one of the gutsiest make-believe people ever is Indiana Jones. Let's watch.

Indiana Jones and the Last Crusade

To show a leap of faith and a demonstration of true guts, play a clip from Indiana Jones and the Last Crusade. *Begin the clip at about 1 hour, 46 minutes, 55 seconds when Indy stands before a chasm. End the clip when Indy crosses the invisible bridge.*

Indy took his step of faith with 100 percent commitment. Following God takes 100 percent commitment, guts, and a willingness to get off our buts. What are our buts? They're excuses that start with "but": "But, God, I can't stand strong. People will think I'm a dork"; "But, God, I just want to have fun in my life right now. It's not my thing to feed the poor"; "But, God, if I hang out

Leadership Tip

As students arrive, play an extreme video, like cool stunts from a Jackie Chan movie. Or at least play some extreme music, like *The Fundamental Elements of Southtown* album by the Christian group P.O.D. If you use a Jackie Chan movie, let students know that he does his own stunts.

with that outcast, I'll lose friends." And the list goes on.

Let's look at what it takes to get off our buts and live for God with guts.

The Message

Key Point #1: G = Give it all to God—he owns you!

"But I want to do my own thing—God'll mess up my thing!" God's whole thing is to mess up your thing because he has something way better. God will not settle for half of our lives or half of our hearts—he wants it all! He created our lives, he purchased them with the blood of his son, Jesus, and besides, we gave our lives to him. Christianity is 100 percent commitment.

Read or summarize Luke 1:11-17; Matthew 3:1-11; and Mark 6:17-29 in that order.

John the Baptist was probably the freakiest "Jesus freak" there ever was. He dressed in animal skins, had long hair, lived in the desert, ate locusts and honey, and he preached hard stuff, telling people to stop sinning and to repent, warning them of hell. John was 100 percent committed. To John anything less than 100 percent commitment was zero. For John it was all or nothing—if you can't run with the big dogs, stay on the porch.

Let's see why this makes sense.

One Half = Zero

Display the items you brought that were chopped in half (and rendered unusable). Make the point that having half of these items is as good as having nothing—they can't fulfill what they were created to do. Then ask:

• How is a halfway commitment to Christ like these items?

• Why won't God settle for less from us and let us run our own lives? make our own choices? decide what's right and wrong on our own?

Polycarp (A.D. 70–155)

Tell students the following true story.

When the Christian church was still very young, Polycarp gained a reputation as a man who stood up for truth and for Christ. Less than eighty years after Jesus died, Polycarp was named the bishop of Smyrna—the man who would have to lead the Christians of the city through the Roman persecution. Despite the hatred and opposition Polycarp faced for leading the church and spreading the gospel, he remained faithful to the call God had given him. The citizens of Smyrna couldn't bear to hear the bold teachings and challenges of Polycarp's Christianity. So they pushed for his arrest.

Three days before he was arrested, Polycarp had a vision. While praying for the early church, he saw his pillow burst into flames…He told his friends he would be burned alive for the sake of the gospel.

When the authorities arrived to arrest Polycarp, Polycarp met the men, served them a meal, and willingly went with them to face the proconsul—the Roman governor. The proconsul interrogated and threatened Polycarp because Christianity was seen as a heretical and godless cult by the Romans. Christians were seen as atheists because they didn't believe in the Roman gods.

"Swear by the genius of Caesar," demanded the proconsul, "Repent (and) say 'Away with the atheists.' "

"Away with the atheists," Polycarp declared after waving his hands at the crowd.

"Swear, and I will release you; curse the Christ," returned the proconsul.

"Eighty-six years I served him, and he has done me no wrong; how can I blaspheme my king who has saved me?" answered Polycarp...

"I will make you be consumed by fire if you don't repent," answered the proconsul.

"You threaten the fire that burns for an hour and in a little while is quenched; for you know not of the fire of judgment to come, and the fire of the eternal punishment reserved for the ungodly. But why do you delay? Bring what you will," answered Polycarp...

The angry mob collected wood and prepared to nail him to a stake. Polycarp assured the crowd that nails weren't necessary and that God would help him to stay in the burning wood without moving. The mob lit the fire and...Polycarp died a faithful father and martyr of the Christian church. (Excerpted from *Character Counts!* by Karl Leuthauser.)

Polycarp was totally sold out and knew that he belonged to God. Even his life was not his own. What are the inward and outward signs that someone is living for God 100 percent? 50 percent? *Get some responses from students.*

God owns us, so we must commit 100 percent of our lives to him.

Key Point #2: U = Unleash yourself into the Unknown.

"But if I give myself to God 100 percent, I'll be doing stuff I know I'll hate, or I'll end up ministering to Pygmies in Africa!" Such an attitude betrays a kind of low level of trust in God, but it's an attitude he will still work with if he needs to. Let's look at how some people imagine they can find God's will.

God, Incorporated

Have your actors perform the skit "God, Incorporated" (pp. 101-102), then lead a short discussion.

- So is this how finding God's will works? Explain.
- How was this portrayal of God like how many people imagine God?
- What advice would you give Sarah?
- What does it take to find and follow God's will? Explain.

Summarize Exodus 3:1—4:17; 5:1-5; 7:14—11:9; 12:1-42. Emphasize Moses' occupation as a shepherd, his calling, his boldness before Pharaoh, and his leading the people of Israel out of Egypt and slavery. Mention, but do not discuss, the ten plagues (Exodus 7:14—11:9) and the Passover (Exodus 12:1-28).

Moses thought he knew what he could do and what he would be best at—being a lonesome shepherd in the desert. But then a God unknown to him spoke to him a calling beyond perhaps his wildest dream. Initially incredulous and doubtful of his calling, Moses had the guts to follow this unknown God. Only then was he given the full vision, guidance, and power he needed to fulfill God's call—leading an entire nation out of slavery, into freedom, and to a promised land.

God placed in you the passions of your heart, the stuff you love to do, and the coolest dream you can imagine. He knows what will bring you ultimate satisfaction, joy, and fulfillment in life, though you may not even know it yet. The God who created you and planned out your days right down to how many breaths you take a day won't steer you wrong and make you commit your life to something you ultimately hate. To have guts, you must be willing to step into the unknown with only God leading you to do what you've never imagined.

Key Point #3: T = Tackle Titanic challenges.

"But what if I fail at stuff God wants me to do? I'll look like a dork!" Good question. Let's look at someone who took on a titanic challenge.

Summarize 1 Samuel 17.

David was a harp-playing shepherd, minding his own business, doing things most people would conclude are menial. Then, while bringing food to his brothers in the army, he heard the taunts of the giant Goliath. As other men shook in their boots and ran from Goliath, David just shouted, "Who is this uncircumcised Philistine that he should defy the armies of the living God?" (verse 26b).

He won no friends for that statement. His older brother got on his case and tried to put him in his place. But David, who was just a boy, won the heart of a nation when he used five stones and a sling to slay the giant who taunted them.

You may have people in your life telling you what you can't be and what you can't do. Maybe you tell yourself defeatist stuff like that. Believing it will keep you ordinary and safely away from being great.

Defy your critics. Take on a titanic challenge for God that's so big there's no question God helped you do it. How well do you face challenges? Let's see.

Change-Catch Challenge

Have students pair up. Distribute ten pennies to each pair. Partners should take turns stacking five pennies on the backs of their hands then flipping their hands quickly enough to catch the pennies. If students do well, they should try stacking two stacks of five and then see how well they do. If this is too easy for the group, give each pair ten more pennies so students can make four stacks of five on the backs of their hands. Then lead a short discussion.

- How eagerly did you take on this relatively small challenge? Why?
- What did you learn about yourself through this activity?
- Do you welcome or fear new challenges? Why?
- If you welcomed challenges, how would you change for the better?

Then just do it! Change right now. Take on a challenge for God. Maybe you really feel you need to read your Bible regularly. Read three chapters a day, starting today. Where is the place you have feared serving but know others have served there? Look into ways to serve there today. Who's the last person with whom you would consider sharing Christ? Share Christ with that person tomorrow.

Leadership Tip

If you have a large group, call ten "brave and tough" volunteers to come forward and do this activity as the rest of the group watches. Revise the discussion accordingly.

Take on titanic challenges and be forever changed. You lose 100 percent of the games you don't play. You miss 100 percent of the shots you don't take. You fail at 100 percent of the things you don't try. With God, failure is not fatal. Life is a learning experience.

Key Point #4: S = Seize the Super-Size opportunities.

"But hey, I just want to have a good time right now. I'll follow God's will tomorrow!" In regard to opportunity, there may be no tomorrow. If you miss out, you miss out. Opportunities do pass people by, and people do live with lifelong regrets over missed opportunities. Today is the day to obey and follow God! Let's look at some folks who obeyed and followed God and some who didn't.

Summarize Numbers 13:1–14:40.

In this account Joshua and Caleb seized a super-size opportunity. Sent out with ten other Israelites to spy on the promised land, Joshua and Caleb boldly went forth with the other spies and observed intimidating people in a fruitful land.

While the other spies floundered in fear, only Joshua and Caleb seized the opportunity to lead the Israelites boldly into God's will. Only they had the faith and guts to follow God and take the land he had promised. The other ten spies later led a rebellion and were struck down by a plague. Of the twelve spies, only Joshua and Caleb entered the promised land.

Sometimes opportunity can be a disguised door. It looks like something too hard, something we're not good at, or something we wouldn't like. When opportunities arise for us to show some guts and leadership in faith, to inspire people to stand for God, and to take God at his Word, we must do it. We, too, have the opportunity to lead people into the promised land.

The Sandlot

To make a good point about opportunities and why people miss them, play a clip from The Sandlot. *Begin the video at 1 hour, 15 minutes, 00 seconds when Babe Ruth comes out of Benny's closet to help him figure out how to retrieve a lost baseball. End the clip at about 1 hour, 17 minutes, 00 seconds when Babe Ruth takes the Henry Aaron baseball card.*

Keepin' It Real!

Share with students a time you were very reluctant to take an opportunity to do something big you had never tried before, whether or not you took the opportunity, and what you learned from the experience.

Closing Challenge

So let go of your buts and follow God with G.U.T.S. He will lead you to your "promised land" of being everything he created you to be.

Commitment Cores

Have students form groups of two or three to discuss these questions:

• What are some buts that you see holding people back from finding and obeying God's will in their lives?

• What are some buts that are holding you back in your walk with God? from finding God's will for your life?

• What one thing will you do today to let go of these buts and follow God with even more guts?

See www.youthministry.com/family_devos for an activity-packed family devotion that you can download for free and copy for your students' parents.

Have group members pray for one another according to what was shared in each group. Then pray that all group members would become the truly unique people God has designed them to be.

Reality Bite

Find a risky activity for your group to do together. For example, on a Friday night, go as a group to share your faith with other teenagers in the parking lot of a local movie theater. Go to a crowded square or public park in your area, and hold up a "Free Prayer" sign, offering to pray for people's needs. Do something really gutsy.

God, Incorporated

Characters

Man at desk: Supposed representative for God, very stiff and annoying

Sarah Zimbloski: A young girl eager to know God's will for her life

Setting and Props

Place desk at center stage with a big sign on front that says, "God, Incorporated." A man should be sitting behind the desk, facing the audience, busily writing when Sarah comes in. The desk should have a thick stack of papers on one side, a phone on the other, and a chair in front of it.

(Sarah enters from the side, being careful not to turn her back to the audience. She clears her throat and sits in the chair.)

Sarah: Um, hello.

Man at desk: And your name is...?

Sarah: Sarah, Sarah Zimbloski.

Man at desk: Is that with a "C" or a "K"?

Sarah: *(Flustered)* That's Sarah with an "S" and Zimbloski with a "Z."

Man at desk: And you are here because...?

Sarah: I want to know God's awesome plan for my life.

Man at desk: And God should stop everything to help you because...?

Sarah: Well...uh...I want God's will for my life. So I thought...

Man at desk: Ahem, yeah, well, here. *(Hands Sarah the big, thick stack of papers.)* Fill this out completely.

Sarah: Whoa! Isn't there a quicker way? You know, you pray, God speaks, then you know what you're supposed to do?

Man at desk: Yeah, well, ya know, that's just not the way it happens today. We did a study and found God's time could be better utilized elsewhere.

Sarah: Sooo, now it's all done by questionnaire? Well, I'm not...

Man at desk: OK, OK. We'll do the short form interview.

Sarah: Short form...I like the sound of that!

Man at desk: (*Sarcastically*) Whatever's *convenient* for *you*. Name's Blimpkowski?

Sarah: That's Zimbloski...um, with a "K"...just kidding, "Z."

Man at desk: Do you prefer Burger King or McDonald's?

Sarah: Ooh, charbroiled—Burger King!

Man at desk: Do you prefer Christina Aguilera or Mariah Carey?

Sarah: Neither!

Man at desk: MTV (*rolls eyes*) or opera (*smiling*)?

Sarah: No question, MTV!

Man at desk: Ahem...Any talents, hobbies, or special skills?

Sarah: Well, I love ministering to junior highers; I play the piano; I paint; I love to pray; I love running my own Web site and chat rooms for young teens; I...

Man at desk: (*Closes and opens hand in a chatting motion.*) Chat, chat, chat. Who am I? I'm Sarah Blimpkowski, and I just *love* to talk about myself!

Sarah: But you asked...

Man at desk: Which are better: *Star Trek* movies or *Star Wars* movies?

Sarah: Oh, that's easy, *Star Wars*.

Man at desk: Hmm. Well, that's all we need...Now let's make a quick call to the man upstairs. (*Dials phone, pauses, and suddenly sits up straight.*) Good morning, Sir, beautiful sunrise this morning...Oh, my pleasure...So who's winning? You? Not surprised...Uh-huh...I have a Sarah Limpkowski here...

Sarah: That's Zimbloski...tell him I love ministering to junior highers!

Man at desk: Shh!...Oh no, Sir, I didn't mean you, Sir...Oh, five-foot-something, likes *Star Wars*, seems OK in the brains department, so...well, relatively speaking... (*to Sarah*) OK with hot climates?

Sarah: Well, yeah, but...

Man at desk: (*To phone*) No problem! Uh-huh...OK...well, you show them who's boss, Boss. (*Laughs loudly.*)...Thanks for your time. (*Hangs up phone. Turns to Sarah.*) You will go to Sri Lanka as a sandal maker.

Sarah: But I don't even own sandals...I *hate* crafts...I can't do this.

Man at desk: It's a sandal maker in Sri Lanka or nothing.

Sarah: I knew it! I just knew that I would end up doing what I hate if I followed God. Well, I guess I'll take nothing.

Man at desk: Suit yourself! God bless you!

(*Sarah leaves quickly.*)

17. Forgiveness for Free (for Real!)

Topics

Forgiveness, grace, Christlike love for others

Scripture Base

Matthew 6:14-15; Mark 11:24-25; Luke 15:11-32; Ephesians 4:32; Colossians 3:12-14

The Point

Forgiveness is God's grace and gift to us, and it should be our gift to others.

Stuff You'll Need

TV and VCR, the movie *Tommy Boy* (Paramount Pictures), newsprint, markers, masking tape, copies of the drama "The Death Sentence"
(p. 108)

Preparation

Several days before the session, find four volunteers to act out the drama "The Death Sentence." They should practice the skit several times. Instruct them to perform the skit during the Closing Challenge, interrupting you as you say, "But no matter what or who we face, we can and must forgive…"

Before the session, write the Commitment Cores questions on a chalkboard or a sheet of newsprint.

Introduction

How many of you have ever been *really* glad to have been forgiven by someone? Find a partner and tell him or her about it. *Allow students a minute or two to share. Then have a volunteer or two share with the group.*

When was the last time you found it a little difficult to forgive? Let's look at someone struggling with this…

Tommy Boy

To show a humorous example of how difficult forgiveness can be at times, play a clip from Tommy Boy. Begin the video at 59 minutes, 50 seconds when the hood flies up on the car. End the clip at 1 hour, 2 minutes, 5 seconds when Tommy says, "I knew it!"

Sometimes forgiveness can seem like the hardest thing to do, but it's never impossible. Let's look at that today.

The Message

Key Point #1: Forgiveness—the attitude

Read or summarize Luke 15:11-32.

This father obviously was a man who maintained a forgiving attitude. His son had asked for an early inheritance ("Gee dad, I can't wait for you to die…how's 'bout giving me my inheritance so I can be on my way?"). He left with the cash and lived a foolish lifestyle. He returned home with nothing, so afraid of what he would find, willing to do anything just to live as one of his father's servants. But what did he find? His father, running to him, filled with love, willing to forgive, rejoicing over his son.

To maintain a forgiving attitude, keep a few things in mind: First, remember that the enemy of close friendships is Satan, and only he will be happy if conflict destroys a relationship. Second, our desire to prosper in and preserve a relationship must outweigh the desire to win an argument, be proved right, or demand our rights.

We must, with the help of God, maintain a forgiving attitude.

Key Point #2: Forgiveness—the action

Read Luke 15:20-24.

Forgiveness is proved with actions, specific actions motivated by true humility and love. This father didn't just tell his youngest son he was forgiven; he took action (hugged and kissed him, put a robe on him, and rejoiced over him). We, too, must put our forgiveness into action.

For-Real Forgiveness

Tape pages of newsprint together to create a big banner. Have students work together to write on the banner as many ways to forgive as possible, such as "I will always love you, no matter what!" and "Give a big bear hug and a gentle kiss on the brow." To prompt ideas, you may have to list specific offenses. After several minutes, lead a short discussion.

• Tell us of a time you really needed forgiveness from someone and that person gave it to you. How did that feel?

• Tell of a time someone really needed your forgiveness and you gave it to that person. How did that feel?

• What's the coolest thing someone has ever done for you or said when you've asked for forgiveness?

Display the banner on the wall, and encourage group members to look at the banner for suggestions of ways they can show forgiveness to others.

Key Point #3: Forgiveness—the gift

Read Ephesians 4:32.

God has given us a free gift of forgiveness. That is, it costs us nothing, but it cost him dearly. Jesus died for our sins. We then must also give forgiveness as a gift—freely—to those who have wronged us and sinned against us.

Keepin' It Real!

Share with group members about a time you weren't so forgiving and how God has helped you to become more forgiving. Really encourage them with the fact that they, too, can change.

Over the Line

Have students stand at one end of your room. Read the statements below, describing sins someone has committed. As you read each one, students should either step forward if they would immediately forgive the person, stay where they are if they would forgive the person eventually, or take one step back if they don't see themselves forgiving the person.

- Someone mispronounces your name over the school intercom, causing some embarrassment.

- Someone bumps into you in the hallway, knocking your books to the floor. The person didn't even try to step to the side.

- Someone cuts you off or tailgates you in traffic.

- Someone spreads false rumors about you, which negatively affect your reputation and your Christian witness.

- Someone runs into your car. The driver was talking on a cellphone and is still on the phone when she walks over to you to exchange information.

- Your youth director commits a sin for which he must resign from the church. Your non-Christian friends leave the youth group as a result. Your youth pastor asks for forgiveness from group members.

- You find out that your younger sister's ex-boyfriend was abusive to her, even physically beating her at times. For some reason he asks for your forgiveness.

- You're falsely accused of a felony, and you serve ten years in prison from age nineteen to twenty-nine. The witness against you later comes forward, saying he lied, and you're released from prison. The witness asks for your forgiveness.

- A close friend of the family molests you when you're a young teenager. Three years later, the person asks for your forgiveness.

- Someone murdered one of your family members. He laughed about the killing then, but now the murderer is on death row and is asking for your forgiveness.

Lead a short discussion.

- Which of these people would you find most difficult to forgive? Why?

- How quickly would Jesus have forgiven each of these people?

- Do you ever struggle with the idea that even a mass murderer could ask for God's forgiveness and be forgiven if he or she is truly repentant? Explain.

- How can God help us forgive?

Leadership Tip

If group members are responding to every question with a "quick to forgive" response, feel free to add further detail to make the sins in the statements even more horrendous.

God can help us, through his Holy Spirit, to forgive anyone of anything, which frees others from the condemnation of their sin and frees us to love with an unlimited love. Forgiving others frees us from the restraints of pain, bitterness, and revenge. In perhaps no other way, we can be more like God when we forgive others.

And what a great gift forgiveness is to share.

Read Matthew 6:14-15. This passage tells us our relationship with God will stay strong and open as we forgive others.

Read Mark 11:24-25. This passage tells us our prayers will be effective as we forgive.

Read Colossians 3:12-14. This passage tells us to forgive because we've been forgiven by God. We must freely give the forgiveness we have so freely received.

Forgiveness for All

Read the following true story.

Corrie ten Boom was a very ordinary Dutch woman. That is, until the Nazis occupied the Netherlands during World War II. Corrie and her family refused to ignore the atrocities that were taking place against their Jewish neighbors. So they opened their home to hide Jewish families from the German Gestapo—the secret police.

A fellow Dutchman turned the ten Booms in to the Gestapo. As a result, Corrie and her sister were taken to Ravensbruck—a women's death camp operated by the Nazis...At Ravensbruck, Corrie and her sister, Betsy, endured forced labor, rat-infested and unheated barracks, malnutrition, disease, and physical abuse. Corrie lost her sister to the Nazi camp.

Despite the awful conditions at Ravensbruck, Corrie led Bible studies and prayer meetings. She even shared scarce food and much-needed medical supplies with the other prisoners. Then miraculously, Corrie was released from Ravensbruck on a clerical error—one week before the rest of the women in her age group were exterminated.

After the war ended, Corrie went back to Ravensbruck to share the gospel...She spoke of God's forgiveness, encouraging the people to accept God's gift. After she had finished speaking at one meeting, she found herself face to face with one of the guards from Ravensbruck. The man had been one of the most despicable and cruel people she had encountered in the camp. He extended his hand to Corrie, seeking the forgiveness she talked about and offered.

"It could not have been many seconds that he stood there," Corrie recalled. "But to me it seemed hours as I wrestled with the most difficult thing I ever had to do." While wrestling with her pain and remembering the loss of her sister, she prayed. Then Corrie forced her hand into the hand of the guard. And Jesus gave her the strength to forgive. She began to feel overwhelmed with joy and freedom as she said, "I do forgive you, brother. With all my heart."

(Excerpted from *Character Counts!* by Karl Leuthauser.)

Closing Challenge

I pray that we're never face to face with someone who is involved in the suffering and resultant death of a loved one, but no matter what or who we face, we can and must forgive...

The Death Sentence

Have your actors interrupt your last sentence and perform the drama "The Death Sentence" (p. 108). After they've performed it, lead a short discussion.

• Did this skit make you think differently of Jesus' death on the cross? If so, how?

• Why are you grateful Jesus took your place? What difference has Jesus made in your life?

• How can comparing our relatively minor persecutions and pain with what Jesus suffered help us to be more forgiving?

Commitment Cores

Have students form groups of two or three to discuss these questions:

• What is your initial reaction to this message?

• Are you a forgiving person? Explain.

• How could you be more forgiving?

• Who do you most need to forgive right now? Why?

• What one thing will you do this week to forgive this person?

Have group members pray for those in their groups according to what was shared. Lead the group in a prayer of thanksgiving to God for his forgiveness and for Jesus' sacrifice on the cross for us. Ask for God's strength and power to forgive others as he has forgiven you.

Reality Bite

Have group members perform "The Death Sentence" for kids in grades four to six in your church. They should then offer a teaching about forgiveness and how to deal with people who are mean to them.

You might also do a study with students on crucifixion as a form of execution. While emphasizing the physical pain of crucifixion, also remember to bring out the emotional and spiritual trauma of it for Jesus, emphasizing how Christ's love and the "joy set before him" helped him to endure the cross.

Family Devotion Online!

See www.youthministry.com/family_devos for an activity-packed family devotion that you can download for free and copy for your students' parents.

The Death Sentence

This drama is one you can simply have actors improvise rather than follow the script word for word.

This would be most effective and more realistic.

Characters
Guard 1: Rough and tough type, wearing matching clothes with Guard 2
Guard 2: Same as Guard 1
Jesus: Should be dressed in clothes a modern teenager would wear
Prisoner: Should be someone with strong dramatic ability

Props
A chair made up to look like an electric chair, a strobe light (optional), a CD with rumbling sound effects (optional), CD player

Setting
Have the "electric chair" set up on the side of the stage farthest from where the Guards and Prisoner will enter.

(Right as leader says "but no matter what or who we face, we can and must forgive…," lights should be dimmed if possible, and Guards should enter quickly, leading the Prisoner. Jesus should trail behind them. Lines are spoken over one another to help get across confusion.)

Prisoner: *(Screaming)* I don't wanna die! I don't wanna die!

Guards 1 and 2: *(Yelling)* Shut up! Keep moving! You're getting what you deserve.

Prisoner: Please, somebody help me! Somebody stop them! Save me! Save me! Save me!

Guards 1 and 2: Shut up, punk! Don't make this harder than it has to be! Keep moving!

(Guards and Prisoner reach the chair, and the Guards pantomime strapping in his arms, legs, and head while he continues to yell.)

Prisoner: No way! This is it! I don't wanna die! I don't wanna die!

Guards 1 and 2: Shut up! Shut up! Nobody wants to hear you!

Prisoner: *(Notices Jesus coming up behind the Guards.)* Hey, man! Help me! Who are you, man? Help me!

(Guards back away. Jesus comes right up to the Prisoner and loosens his arms, legs, and head.)

Prisoner: Who are you, man? What are you doing? I mean—they're gonna get you, man.

(Jesus pulls the man out of the chair.)

Prisoner: What the…? What are you doing? Are you crazy? What's wrong with you, man?

(Jesus sits in the chair. The Guards grab the Prisoner by the arm and hold him back. He is trying to run to the chair.)

Prisoner: What's he doing? That should be me, man! That should be me! Jesus, it should be me, not you!

(Flicker room lights or run the strobe light. Play loud, rumbling sound effects. Jesus should be slumped in the chair.)

Prisoner: It should've been me, man! It should've been me…

Perfectly...Imperfect!

Topics

Perfection, flaws and weaknesses, patience

Scripture Base

Matthew 5:43-48; 2 Corinthians 12:9-10; Ephesians 4:2-6; Philippians 1:6; Colossians 1:28-29

The Point

We must respond to the weaknesses and imperfections of others and ourselves with Christlike grace and affirm one another's strengths, gifts, and good qualities.

Stuff You'll Need

TV and VCR, the movie *My Best Friend's Wedding* (Columbia/TriStar Pictures), copies of the skit "Will the Real Crissy Please Stand Up?" (pp. 114-115), bubble solution with wand, newsprint, markers, CD player, lively Christian music (optional)

Preparation

Before the session, recruit three actors for the "Will the Real Crissy Please Stand Up?" skit. They should practice for an hour or more to be fully prepared.

Write the Commitment Cores questions on a chalkboard or a sheet of newsprint.

Introduction

You know, sometimes we're just not as sharp or bright as we hope to be. Let me illustrate.

Possibly the World's Dumbest Criminals

• After robbing a home and placing the stolen merchandise in his car, the robber decided to take a bubble bath, fell asleep, and awoke to be greeted by the homeowner—and the police.

• A man stripped naked to rob a bank, thinking that without distinctive clothing he would be harder to catch. Deputies easily spotted him.

• A woman whose car was stolen mentioned to police that she had a car phone. The policeman called the thief on the car phone and said he had seen the ad in the paper, which was a lie, and wanted to buy the car. They arranged to meet and the thief was arrested.

• A couple out camping returned to their motor home to find a man vomiting in the bushes. He had attempted to siphon gas from their tank but hooked up to the holding tank for the toilet instead (adapted from www.dumbcriminalacts.com).

Turn to a partner and share a not-so-bright thing you've done lately. Then share your "least favorite imperfection" in others. *Allow students about three minutes to share, then have courageous* souls share what they told their partners.

Imperfection is all over the place. In fact, we're all perfect in one way—perfect in our imperfection. Think about that for a minute. *Smile.* Seems like it would be in our best interest to learn to deal better with the imperfections of others as well as our own. Let's look at that today.

The Message

Key Point #1: Imperfect people...ya gotta love 'em.

Read Ephesians 4:2-6.

God loves all of us imperfect people the same. He calls us to humility, to gentleness, to patience, and to bear with one another in love. We can't let love truly live unless we love unrestrained and without limit—not forcing anyone for some reason to "qualify" for our love. Love no matter what.

My Best Friend's Wedding

To show a great example of accepting imperfection in someone, play a clip from the movie My Best Friend's Wedding. Let students know that Julianne is trying to steal her long-term ex-boyfriend and best friend, Michael, from his fiancé, Kim, days before the wedding. After discovering a certain weakness Kim has, Julianne volunteers her to do something. Let's see what that weakness is.

Begin the clip at 24 minutes, 40 seconds when Julianne volunteers Kim to sing a song. End the clip at 27 minutes, 30 seconds when Kim and Michael kiss.

• How would you have felt if you had been Kim in this situation? Why?

• What would you have done? Kept singing? Quit? Why?

• How is the way Julianne set Kim up for embarrassment like or unlike how you see people respond to the weaknesses and imperfections in others? Explain.

Didn't Michael deal with Kim's "imperfection" pretty well? Yep, sometimes we really have to be willing to accept some imperfections in those closest to us, in those we love. We're called to love others in spite of their weaknesses.

That's where the struggle comes in. We struggle with the imperfections of others and don't handle them so gracefully. We get stuck on them, get turned off, get angry, become impatient, let them irk us, and find it hard to look past a person's weaknesses and love that person as Christ has called us to.

If we're not careful, we can become someone who sees only the bad in others, one who dwells on the imperfections of others, one who finds it difficult to encourage and love unconditionally.

Bubble Busters!

Suddenly begin blowing bubbles over group members' heads. If you brought some lively music, play it as you blow the bubbles and group members chase them. Notice that the first reaction of most students will be to try to pop the bubbles. If anyone is trying to catch and hold the bubbles, take special note of that. Blow bubbles for about a minute. Then stop, and instruct group members to try to catch bubbles in their hands without popping them. Then lead a short discussion.

- What was the reaction of most of us when the bubbles went flying all over the place? Why?

- Was it harder to pop bubbles or to catch them without popping them?

- How was our reaction to the bubbles (popping them or trying to hold them) like some people's reactions to others and their imperfections?

The first reaction for most of us would be to pop the bubbles. After all, popping bubbles is much easier than catching them and holding them. The way people often treat one another is very similar. Too many of us are bubble busters. We find it too natural and easy to burst people's bubbles by treating them unkindly or by limiting our love to the deserving or "together" people. Love takes effort sometimes. We don't just do it if we feel it; we're to be loving because that's the right thing to do—what God calls us and empowers us to do. Let's be bubble makers, not bubble busters.

Let's face it, this world is fresh out of perfect people since Jesus shed his human skin. Nobody's left but us imperfect folks. So we have to love one another in spite of (and sometimes because of) our imperfections. Imperfect people…ya gotta love 'em!

Key Point #2: Imperfect you…ya gotta love ya!

Will the Real Crissy Please Stand Up?

Have actors perform the skit (pp. 114-115). Then lead a short discussion.

- Do you think most people are pretty insecure or not? Why?

- If you were Crissy's friend, what would you have said or done to help Crissy?

Read Philippians 1:6.

God has begun an incredible work in you—begun! He's got *lots* left to do with you. He loves you too much to let you stay the way you are!

Read 2 Corinthians 12:9-10.

How do you think our weaknesses can show God's strength? *Await response.* Our weaknesses and imperfections are things God can work with. God loves us no matter what our weaknesses and imperfections are. Sometimes our weaknesses can limit how we see ourselves.

How Many?

Have students fully extend their right arms in front of them and stretch out their four fingers as if looking at their nails or trying to tell someone "stop." Ask them how many fingers they see. They should say four. Then have them look past their hands and focus on something beyond their fingers (perhaps a wall or something else). They should see what looks like eight fingers.

- Why did what we saw change?

- What can we learn from this as we see ourselves and our weaknesses and imperfections?

We must accept our weaknesses and delight in the opportunities they provide for us to see God's strength, but we must also look past them. If we focus on our weaknesses, we can limit

Keepin' It Real!

Tell students of a time you found it difficult to look past someone's imperfection or weakness but eventually did it (and how you did it).

Keepin' It **Real!**

Tell students of a time you found it difficult to see past your own weaknesses and what happened to change that for you.

ourselves pretty quickly and find it hard to see all the cool, wonderful things about ourselves that God has put in us. We've got to set our sights higher. Imperfect you...ya gotta love ya!

Key Point #3: Nobody's perfect...except Jesus.

Picture Perfect? Part 1

Distribute sheets of newsprint to students along with markers. Students should quickly draw pictures of themselves on the newsprint. These won't be works of art, just quick, basic sketches. After two or three minutes, have them circle areas of themselves that they feel are weak or imperfect. If they would like to note any inner weaknesses, such as "I'm too shy," they should simply write them on the bodies of their self-portraits. You may want students to note only three to five weaknesses about themselves. Under each weakness, students should write a way they think God can be strong in them through that weakness. For example, if someone did note that he or she was too shy, that person could also write, "God could use me to quietly share my faith with others through acts of kindness. I don't have to talk, I just have to love with God's help." Have some students share what they wrote if they feel comfortable. Then ask:

• Was this easy or difficult for you? Why?

Read Matthew 5:43-48.

So we're cool with being imperfect. But what about this verse that challenges us to be perfect as God is perfect? What do you think this means? *Encourage student response.* One thing is clear from this passage—it's calling us to be unlimited and unconditional in our love. In this way we can be "perfect" like God, through God.

This doesn't happen instantly; in fact, we never really arrive, but we become progressively more like Christ. We become more perfect in our love as we follow him, draw close to him, and love him with all our heart.

This, then, is our standard—not instant perfection but the process of growing toward being like Christ. We should settle for nothing less but, at the same time, understand and accept that we're in process and we require patience—as do others who know Christ.

Read Colossians 1:28-29.

Perfect means *becoming* mature and complete. We become more like Jesus and more perfectly loving as we grow up and grow closer to him. Nobody's perfect except Jesus. We're perfectly imperfect. But when we love, we're at our best, we look the most like him, and we're probably as perfect as we'll be while on this earth.

Closing Challenge

Picture Perfect? Part 2

Have students write their names at the tops of their self-portraits they drew earlier. Have students sit in a circle and pass the self-portraits around. Group members should write on each self-portrait all the ways that person is like Jesus. If they like something about the person, they should draw a star on the portrait or on the paper and write what they like so much. It's very important that students write on as many self-portraits as possible and make sure no one is left without stars or affirmation. After about three minutes, have everyone return the self-portraits to their owners. Give students a minute or two to read what others wrote. Then lead a short discussion.

• How did you like looking past our weaknesses for a moment to affirm one another's strengths and qualities?

• What was the most meaningful thing someone wrote about you?

Well, none of us is perfect—God is still working on us. And that's pretty exciting. Meanwhile let's cut one another some slack and forgive our weaknesses, overlook the imperfections, and look for what there is to love in one another.

Commitment Cores

Have students form groups of two or three to discuss these questions:

• Show your self-portrait to your group. What are some of the things that stand out most in what people wrote? Why?

• Without naming the person, who is someone you know with an imperfection or weakness to which you don't respond well? Explain.

• What's one imperfection or weakness of yours that you really wish you could change with God's help? Why?

• What one thing will you do to respond more positively to the person you previously mentioned and his or her imperfection or weakness? *Group members should help one another brainstorm actions to take.*

• What one thing will you do to respond more positively to your imperfection or weakness? *Group members should help one another brainstorm actions to take.*

Have students pray for one another in their groups according to what each person shared. Close by praying that each person will be patient and loving toward the imperfections of others as well as his or her own imperfections.

Reality Bite

It would be good for you and your students to spend some time with "imperfect" people, those with physical or mental disabilities. Go with small groups of students to spend some time with such special people, preferably people your students know from church and will see on a regular basis in the future. They can do things such as spend a few hours at a local park or do something they enjoy at people's homes. In summertime they could work at a camp for children with special needs. Or around Christmastime your group can sing Christmas carols and bring gifts for people with special needs. Group members can realize that being "imperfect" isn't so bad and that even imperfect people like themselves can love others.

Family Devotion Online!

See www.youthministry.com/family_devos for an activity-packed family devotion that you can download for free and copy for your students' parents.

Will the Real Crissy Please Stand Up?

Characters
Crissy: A girl who loves Todd and is madly aware of her imperfections
Beth: Crissy's best friend and primary "reality check"
Todd: A handsome, secure, friendly guy

Props
Table with three chairs, three plates with hamburgers

(Crissy and Beth are sitting at a cafeteria table, facing the audience. They have two plates with hamburgers.)

Crissy: So anyway, I'm sitting there looking at her, asking, "Is *this* what you call a nail job? This was not at all my vision for my nails…"

(Todd enters stage right, seems to be talking to someone.)

Beth: *(Sees Todd.)* Speaking of vision—there he is, Todd Morrow, *your* vision of love.

Crissy: Ohmigosh, you're right…so right. I am such a pathetic loser around him. Before I die I want to say one coherent sentence to Todd Morrow.

(Todd walks toward them.)

Beth: Well, looks like you'll get your chance. Here he comes now.

(He turns away and exits.)

Crissy: Beth, you are such a liar. *(Starts rubbing teeth with finger.)* Is there anything stuck in my teeth? My hair, ohmigosh, it is so gross! My breath…*(Blows into cupped hands, trying to smell breath.)* Is my breath OK? *(Breathes on Beth.)*

Beth: *(Amused, making mock choking noises)* I'd keep my distance!

Crissy: Oh man, I should *not* have worn this outfit—it makes me look fat! Don't you think this outfit makes me look fat?

Beth: No, your face does.

Crissy: Oh, that's good…hey!

Beth: You know I am so kidding…and by the way, Todd's gone.

Crissy: *(Slides down into chair.)* Oh, what a relief!

Beth: You realize, of course, that you are insane or *totally* in love—or something—with this guy? Why can't you just be yourself?

Crissy: I know, I know. You saw me. I was like a pathetic loser even hearing he was in the cafeteria.

(Todd appears again, walking toward them, standing right behind them. He's carrying a plate with a burger on it.)

Crissy: *(Closes her eyes, tilts her head back, and raises her voice.)* I am in love with Todd Morrow, but I would just die if he knew!

Todd: (Ignoring Crissy) Is this seat taken?

(Crissy immediately sits straight up in her chair with a look of horror on her face as Beth laughs. Mouths at Beth, "Why didn't you tell me he was here?")

Beth: No, please, *please* have a seat!

Todd: These mystery meat burgers have got to be the worst!

Crissy: Oh, I know, they're the worst.

Beth: Gee, I thought you said just a minute ago that they were the best...

Crissy: (Kicks Beth under the table.) The lesser of many evils, I said.

Todd: (With mouth full) So have you heard the new CD by the *Nasty Na-Na-Nas?*

Crissy: Oh yeah, I mean, um, who hasn't, you know? It's incredible!

Beth: Don't you mean horrible? Just yesterday you said...

(Crissy kicks Beth under the table again.)

Beth: Ouch!

Crissy: Horribly good, I believe was the phrase you were searching for, Beth.

Todd: (Oblivious, pantomimes watching someone walk by.) Sherry Ott is so pretty but so incredibly insecure. I mean, I'll talk with her and she always asks if I think she's fat, and she holds her hand over her mouth sometimes—like she's self-conscious about her breath or something. If she weren't so insecure, she'd be really attractive. No self-confidence is such a turnoff.

Crissy: I know what you mean. The insecure types are the worst.

Beth: They sure are! (Gives Crissy a hard stare and nods her head in agreement with Todd.)

Todd: That's why I want a self-confident girl who isn't hung up on how she looks, you know, a strong person. Not the needy type.

Crissy: Couldn't have said it better myself...I mean, about girls, I mean guys, I mean, you know, I like girls—guys, I mean...self-confidence...is good.

Beth: You have derailed...

Todd: Oh man, I gotta go! (Stands.) See ya! (Leaves.)

Beth and Crissy: Bye!

Beth: Well, that went well, I thought.

Crissy: (Gently bangs her head on the table as she speaks.) I am so stupid, stupid, stupid. I am such a loser, loser, loser...

Beth: Now which Crissy did Todd see—the psycho pretend woman or the good-looking and has no reason to be insecure Crissy? Hmm. Will the real Crissy *please* stand up?

Crissy: (Still banging head) Loser, loser, loser...

19. Power Prayer

Topics

The Lord's prayer, prayer, intimacy with God

Scripture Base

Matthew 6:5-15; 1 John 4:4

The Point

The Lord's prayer is a powerful pattern for prayer that Jesus modeled for his followers.

Stuff You'll Need

TV and VCR, the movies *The Iron Giant* (Warner Bros.) and *Sister Act* (Touchstone Pictures), can of warm soda, can opener, plastic for the floor, markers, watch with a second hand or timer

Preparation

Before the session, write the Commitment Cores questions on a chalkboard or a sheet of newsprint.

Introduction

The Iron Giant

To have a little fun with "power prayer," play a seemingly forceful "warfare prayer " from the movie The Iron Giant. Let students know that basically the boy in this scene, Hogarth, has discovered a robot that came to Earth in a spaceship. Every part of this robot has a mind of its own. Wandering robot parts are what inspire Hogarth's "impassioned" prayer.

Begin the clip at 28 minutes, 00 seconds when Hogarth's mother asks him, "Would you say grace, please?" End the clip at 29 minutes, 00 seconds when Hogarth says, "I forgot to wash my hands."

Wow, what a truly, truly powerful prayer. If only we all would pray so fervently and with such passion…and if only we all would *avoid* praying like this…

Sister Act

To give an example of how not to pray, show a clip from Sister Act. Share this information to set up the clip: Deloris is in protective custody until she can testify in a mob murder case. The police hide her in a convent as Sister Mary Clarence. Another nun invites Sister Mary Clarence to say the blessing for the meal.

Begin the clip at 22 minutes, 40 seconds when Sister Mary Clarence and the Reverend Mother walk down the hall. End the clip at 24 minutes, 30 seconds when the nuns sit down.

Today we're going to look at power prayer and how to avoid the kinds of prayer we just saw. We'll look at a familiar model for prayer from a different angle to find a truly powerful pattern for daily prayer. It begins with Jesus. Before we go any further, it's important that we understand his attitude toward prayer.

For Jesus prayer was not an "if" thing; it was a "when" thing. If Jesus, the Son of God, needed prayer, how much more do we need prayer? Consider the vital role prayer played in the life of Jesus.

- Jesus made prayer his first order of the day (Mark 1:35).
- Sometimes Jesus prayed through the night (Luke 6:12).
- Jesus prayed before he picked his disciples (Luke 6:13).
- Jesus prayed before he faced death on the cross (Matthew 26:36).

To pray with power, we must lose our casual attitude toward prayer and imitate Jesus. In Matthew 6 Jesus gave us a simple, yet profoundly powerful, pattern for prayer. *Have a student read Matthew 6:5-15.*

The Message

Key Point #1: Honor God and see him as he is.

Read Matthew 6:9-10.

When you begin to pray, worship God! Expressions of worship, praise, and adoration to God should begin our prayers. Such expressions recognize God's position (Father, Almighty God). They remind us of our position under him (his children). Such prayer is a prime, USDA choice opportunity to get to know God. There may be no better way to know God this side of heaven, yet some people still don't take advantage of this tremendous and incredible privilege.

God, a Closed Fist?

Have students pair up. Distribute markers. Have students write on the insides of their hands one or two words that best describe themselves. Instruct them to be very honest, maybe writing something they wouldn't choose to share otherwise.

Then each person should make a tight fist with that hand. At your signal, people should hold out both fists to their partners. With their writing hands, students should try, for thirty (or sixty) seconds, to open their partners' fists.

- How easy was it to find out what your partner had written? Why?
- How is this like the way some people allow others to see who they really are?
- Would you say you're more like a closed fist or an open hand in allowing people to see who you really are?
- Would you say most people consider that getting to know God is like opening a closed fist (someone who's hard to know)? Why or why not?
- To you, is God a closed fist or an open hand? Why?

God wants to be known by people like you and me. He reveals himself and gives countless opportunities even in a single day for people to see him, experience him, and know him.

God doesn't want to play Hide and Seek with us. He isn't hiding from us. He wants us to know him. Christianity is a personal and intimate faith. Christ began the model prayer with "Our Father." The Aramaic word for "father," "abba," literally means "papa." Christ wanted us to remember two key things about our Father. First, God is a loving Father who longs to speak to us and speak into our lives. Second, his will and purposes are better than ours for our lives—far better. When these two beliefs become reality for us, we'll find it difficult to miss our prayer times with God. In daily prayer we must honor God and see him as he is.

Key Point #2: Recognize that you aren't God.

Read Matthew 6:11.

We must humbly acknowledge our complete dependence upon God for all our needs. People are funny. We like to think we're our own gods, in charge of our lives, self-sufficient, self-reliant, self-motivated, self-made—whew, there's a lot of self, self, self there! In reality we have nothing—absolutely nothing—except what God has given us. Not one scrap of food, not one thread of clothing, not one talent or skill, not even one ounce of intelligence—nothing, nada, zip.

There are two key words in this passage: "give" and "daily." God is our daily source for all gain, provision, blessing, and any other good thing. He daily provides for our needs.

Prayer Is Like Air

Turn to your partner. Facing your partner, sit down, hold your breath, and hold your partner's nose shut. Let's see who can hold his or her breath the longest. *Use a watch with a second hand or a timer to track the time.* When you can hold your breath no longer, stand up.

• Describe what is was like to be without air for as long as you were.

• Someone once said that when you're as desperate to pray and connect with God as you were desperate for air, only then is prayer in its proper place in your heart and life. What do you think that person was getting at?

• How might prayer be to our spirits like air is to our bodies?

A necessary attitude for prayer with power is the recognition that without God we have nothing in our lives. He is our source for all that we need. He alone brings us life.

If we don't give God daily recognition that all provision, resource, and blessing ultimately come from him, we open ourselves up to be deceived and to foolishly attribute it all to our own effort or to some earthly institution. We must daily humbly recognize our deep dependence upon God for all our needs.

Key Point #3: Recognize that you *really* are not God.

Read Matthew 6:12.

Jesus died for our sins—he carried the pain and the penalty so we wouldn't have to. We must bring our pain, hurt, and sin before him so we can be delivered and set free and can realize the full benefit of his forgiveness and grace.

We must confess our need for forgiveness and our need of God's help to forgive others—to love them as God loves us.

Key Point #4: Recognize you *really, really* are not God.

Read Matthew 6:13.

Leadership Tip

Those with respiratory problems, like asthma, may not be able to participate in this activity. Instead, they may want to take a slow deep breath and hold it for two or three seconds just to get a little idea of how it feels.

Prayer Is Like Opening up a Can...

Shake the can of warm soda. Hold up the can and the can opener.

Try to figure out the object lesson I'm about to do. How are the "under pressure" contents of this can like the power of God, and how is this can opener like prayer? *Encourage student response as you walk around acting as if you will, at any moment, open the can with the can opener.*

The contents of this can are like the power of God—the most dynamic and powerful force of all—just waiting to be unleashed in the world and in our life situations. Prayer is like "opening up a can" of spiritual power. So if you're feeling kicked around or down in your daily life...open up a can.

You decide if you want to open the can—though not doing so immediately and waiting may be a good illustration that shows how much less fun it is to leave the contents in the can than it is to put a little hole in the top and see all the contents empty out in a few seconds.

It can be easy to be overwhelmed by the wickedness in our world if we don't live in daily awareness that God is stronger than all of it and that his Spirit and his Word live in our hearts. In us is the power to overcome it all.

Read aloud 1 John 4:4, and have students say it aloud with you twice.

Prayer is like a compass. It's a tool God uses to order our lives, adjust our course, and prepare us to overcome the storm waves of life that threaten us. Without his guidance we're adrift and at the mercy of a turbulent, unpredictable, and adversarial world. We must daily pray to recognize that we really, really are not God. We're in desperate need of his guidance, power, and protection.

Closing Challenge

George Mueller—a Man of Faith

Read the following true story for students.

George Mueller lived in the mid-1800's. By the time he was of college age, he was a thief, an ex-con, a liar, a partier, and a womanizer. But in mid-November 1825, as a result of attending a Saturday evening Christian meeting and listening to a sermon, he made a faith commitment to Jesus that turned his life around.

In 1826 George felt inclined to become a missionary. By 1829 he had completed his university courses and set off for London to become a missionary. George Mueller set out to show an unbelieving nation that God was still in control.

He set up schools to teach children and adults to read and write. He supported missionaries all over the world, sending them Bibles and tracts to distribute. How did he do all this? Without ever uttering a word to any human, George would take his needs to God—and God would miraculously provide.

In addition to his missionary efforts, George founded several orphanages to care for poor, abandoned children. These young orphans, who might have been jailed to keep them from begging on the city streets, now had a place to call home—a place where they could have food and clothes and, most important, learn about God's love.

George dedicated his life to caring for these children, and yet he never told anyone about the financial needs of his orphanages—he only told God. And God *always* provided. One great example of God's amazing answers to prayer is the Ashley Down Orphanage. At the time of George's death, the orphanage was caring for about two thousand children in five different buildings. In fact the price of each building was $600,000, which was all provided through answered prayer! George prayed specifically for the needs of his ministry, and God answered; in fact, George proclaimed with confidence that God had been faithful to answer fifty thousand specific requests. (Facts excerpted from http://members .truepath.com/aocommunities/george_mueller.htm.)

Lead a short discussion.

• What is your reaction to George Mueller and his faith?

• How would your life be different if you never shared your needs with anyone and just brought them to God in prayer?

• What does this tell you about the importance of daily prayer and what it can do in our lives?

We must pray with power daily.

Commitment Cores

Have students form groups of two or three to discuss these questions:

• What one word best describes your prayer life? Why?

• How has this message challenged you in your prayer life?

• What one thing could you do differently in your prayer life to pray with power?

Invite students to share prayer requests. As people share, challenge students to really try to take on people's requests as if they were their own. Encourage them to try to feel what the person sharing must be feeling, such as frustration, sadness, burden, or confusion, and try to put themselves in the other person's situation so they can pray for that person from their heart. Close the session by having students take turns praying for the needs that were shared.

Reality Bite

As a special prayer challenge, have seven consecutive evenings of power prayer and praise. This works best during the summer but can work with a motivated group any time of year. Come together for one and a half hours each night for seven days straight. Praise and worship God in song for a half hour, then pray for an hour for the following: the nation and its leader, the state or province and your city or town, your church's leaders, those in your congregation who have needs, and youth group members and the youth group. You may want to provide students with a printed "prayer outline" supplying all the prayer requests. Update the outline daily.

Family Devotion Online!

See www.youthministry.com/family_devos for an activity-packed family devotion that you can download for free and copy for your students' parents.

20. Love Overflow Versus Hate Undertow

Topics

Hatred, love, hardened heart

Scripture Base

Zechariah 7:9-12; Ephesians 4:3-6; 1 John 1:8-9; 2:9; 3:11-12, 14-15

The Point

God has called us to overflow with love toward all people and not get caught in the hate undertow even toward some.

Stuff You'll Need

TV and VCR, the movie *Selena* (Warner Bros.), copies of the "What Would You Do?" handout (p. 126), poster board, markers

Preparation

Before the session, write the Commitment Cores questions on a chalkboard or a sheet of newsprint.

Introduction

Hatred. What comes to mind when I say that word? *Encourage student responses.* Christians who hate. Is this possible? Is it realistic? Why? *Again, encourage student response.* Let's look at some examples of hatred.

Portraits of Hatred/ Portraits of Love

Have group members form three teams. Give each team one of the following assignments below and materials (if needed). Allow students about three minutes to prepare. Then have each team present its work to the group.

Assignment 1—Hate Poster

Materials: poster board, markers

Instructions: Draw the word "hate" on the poster in a way that captures the "personality" of the word. Or draw a present-day example of hatred, such as two protesters on either side of the abortion issue or students walking by another student and whispering, "What a geek!" The whole team must be involved.

Assignment 2—Hate Role-Play

Instructions: Create one or two short skits depicting hatred, such as being rude toward someone of another race, behaving angrily toward an atheist, or cliquing up with other students. The whole team must be involved.

Assignment 3—Hate Freeze Frame

Instructions: Create a freeze frame depicting hatred in some way, such as avoiding or rejecting someone as a geek or a nerd or expressing hateful attitudes toward someone of another race or religion behind the person's back. The whole team must be involved.

When all teams have displayed or performed their work, have them create the same kind of assignment for love. People drawing the poster should flip over their poster board and make a drawing of the word "love." The role-play should end with a loving resolution. The freeze frame should depict love. After everyone presents their new work for the group, lead a short discussion.

• Both hatred and love have many faces. Which face do you see most in our culture, hatred or love? Explain.

• What is our Christian responsibility to our culture in regard to love and hate? Explain.

For the Christian, hatred is not an option. Love has to overflow, and we must avoid the hatred undertow. Let's look at why that is.

The Message

Key Point #1: Hatred allies us with the evil one and destroys lives.

Read 1 John 2:9; 3:11-12, 14-15.

Have you ever wanted to have any connection to Cain? with Satan? Well, just cross a little bridge called hatred, and you can have it. Our hatred puts us in the same state of mind that eventually led Cain to take his brother's life. Hatred was behind the murder of Abel. Hatred murders. It assassinates. If we allow ourselves to hate, it kills our ability to love others and show them kindness.

Hatred is an act of rebellion against what God has called us to do on this earth. We are here to love. When we hate, we not only stop fighting for the right side but ally with the dark side. Hatred can put us under some pretty heavy influence from Satan. It identifies and aligns us with him and the current mean spirit of our culture, just as showing love and kindness identifies and aligns us with God.

Hatred allies us with the evil one who destroys lives. Love shows we are God's children, brings life, and builds lives.

Key Point #2: Hatred hardens our hearts and angers God.

Read Zechariah 7:9-12.

Hatred hardens us. God will try to soften us, but if hatred has gripped our hearts even a little bit, we will stubbornly turn our backs on him or plug our ears to God's voice. This makes God angry. That's not good.

Hatred shuts the door on reconciliation and understanding between races. It labels someone a homosexual rather than someone who deserves to be shown God's love. It makes us selfish and uncaring. Hatred hardens our hearts.

As a result, all the lives we could have touched with God's love remain untouched. All the opportunities to serve and show kindness to others pass us by. All the light we were to shine is snuffed out by the darkness that builds in us. Hatred hardens our hearts and shuts them down, but love softens our hearts and opens us up to be the wonderfully loving people God has called us to be. Hatred hardens our hearts and angers God. Love softens our hearts and pleases God.

Key Point #3: Hate divides Christians.

Read Ephesians 4:3-6.

The Bible is telling us here that we should "make every effort to keep the unity of the Spirit through the bond of peace." Unfortunately this unity of the Spirit is too rarely seen.

For example, some people who call themselves Christians still view people of other races with contempt. And some of the most heated battles between those who claim the name "Christian" usually involve love versus hate.

For example, some say, "We must show love to the person practicing homosexuality" while others say, "We must show wrath to the homosexual." Some say, "We must reconcile the races and come together as one and equal" while others contend, "We are as close as we need to be" and never share the same dinner table or interact socially with those of other races. Some say, "All Christians are one body—we are all part of the same flock" while others contend, "Our denomination's view of faith is the pure one, and practically everyone else's is flawed and in error."

Hatred divides the body while love is our only hope of pulling together the body. The body of Christ (the church) must unite to represent God more perfectly on earth by showing God's love, hope, and salvation to the world.

Key Point #4: Hate blinds us.

Selena

To make a point about the subtle nature of some forms of hatred, show a clip from the movie Selena. Begin the clip at 1 hour, 40 minutes, 00 seconds with a shot of an airplane in flight. End the clip at 1 hour, 41 minutes, 32 seconds when Selena winks at her friend after letting the clerk know she isn't interested in the $800 dress. Then lead a short discussion.

• Where in this clip did you detect some subtle hatred?

Read 1 John 1:8-9.

Ninety-nine percent of people will make the claim "I don't hate anybody," yet they participate in cliques, they exclude from friendship those who are different, they use racist or sexist humor, and they stereotype people of other races. So in the test of life, the true colors often come out. Hatred is simmering just below the surface.

Not Me!

Have students form small groups of two or three. Give each person a copy of the "What Would You Do?" handout (p. 126). Students should read the situations aloud in their small groups. Then each person should take ten seconds to say what his or her response (emotional and physical) would be and why.

After about three minutes, pull the group together again and ask:

• In what ways do you think all of us could be more loving toward others, especially when tested in ways like those you discussed in your small groups?

You may not think this was totally fair and say, "But this gets our initial reaction. If we had a minute to think, we could have done better." Our reactions are truly the indicators to where our hearts are.

Once hatred takes over in our hearts and minds, it can really start affecting our perceptions. Suddenly people who "God dearly loves" become members of a race we don't like, perverts, nerds, geeks, freaks, weirdos, or jerks. And we don't even think twice about it.

Hatred is so subtle that many times we don't even realize we have it. Hatred blinds us and brings darkness to our souls. Love opens our eyes and lets the light of God shine in and through us.

Closing Challenge

As Christians we're gifted with an unlimited capacity to love others if we'll just tap into it. Let's look at one man whose ability to love seems truly unlimited.

Christopher Carrier

Tell students the following true story.

In 1974, at ten years old, Christopher Carrier was abducted from his Miami, Florida bus stop by convicted felon David McAllister, who attacked him with an ice pick, shot him in the head, and left him for dead in the Everglades, an alligator-infested area. He was found six days later by a hunter, dazed and confused, sitting on a rock. Though Christopher was left blinded in one eye and emotionally traumatized for a long time after the abduction and attack, a year or two later he found Christ, and his life was changed.

In 1996, when his attacker was found living in a Miami-area nursing home, Chris went to see him. Though his heart could have been filled with hate and he could have taken revenge in one way or another, Chris faced his attacker with the grace and love of Jesus and extended to McAllister the forgiveness he sought.

For several weeks up until McAllister's death, Chris visited McAllister each day, reading him the Bible, praying with him, and ultimately sharing Christ with him.

If Chris Carrier could love the man who tried to murder him, surely we can, through Christ, love those who have hurt or brought harm to us.

Commitment Cores

Have students form groups of two or three to discuss these questions:

• When have you seen the destruction hatred can bring?

• What is the number one reason Christians shouldn't hate?

• In what ways do people you know struggle with hatred?

• In what one area of your life right now can you choose love over hate?

Have group members pray for one another according to what each person shared. Then close the session in prayer, asking God to help group members get caught in his love overflow instead of the hate undertow.

Reality Bite

Take group members to a local mall. Dispatch them to show love and kindness to as many people as possible (and to keep a list). They may do things like smile at people to see if they smile back, help someone reach an item high on a shelf, say a kind word to a harried clerk, hold the door and greet people as they enter the mall, surrender their places in a food line to other people, and more. Afterward sit and enjoy soft drinks while comparing notes.

Family Devotion Online!

See www.youthministry.com/family_devos for an activity-packed family devotion that you can download for free and copy for your students' parents.

What Would You Do?

• A person who practices homosexual sin calls you a homophobe because you say you believe homosexual activity is a sin.

• Imagine that you're an African-American (if you aren't). You're watching television and a black comedian uses the "n" word. What the person said was funny to you and you laugh. But then you notice white people in the television audience laughing.

• An abortion rights group comes to your campus and does a humorous presentation about safe sex and how to use a condom. They give out condoms. The school will not allow an abstinence presentation.

• You're exiting an elevator into a darkened hallway. An unsmiling person, who is the same sex as you are but a different race, pushes onto the elevator before you can exit, bumping you in the process.

• While driving, you're following an elderly person driving very slowly with her left blinker on for miles. You can't pass her.

• You see two guys hugging and kissing right beside a playground where your little brother and other kids are playing.

• You're an American citizen with no health care. You were just hospitalized. You received a huge bill saying, "Pay today." Just then, on the news, you see a news report of the increasing problem of people from another country slipping into the country illegally. They're given free health care.

Group Publishing, Inc.
Attention: Product Development
P.O. Box 481
Loveland, CO 80539
Fax: (970) 679-4370

Evaluation for
The Top 20 Messages for Youth Ministry

Please help Group Publishing, Inc. continue to provide innovative and useful resources for ministry. Please take a moment to fill out this evaluation and mail or fax it to us. Thanks!

● ● ●

1. As a whole, this book has been (circle one)

not very helpful   very helpful

1   2   3   4   5   6   7   8   9   10

2. The best things about this book:

3. Ways this book could be improved:

4. Things I will change because of this book:

5. Other books I'd like to see Group publish in the future:

6. Would you be interested in field-testing future Group products and giving us your feedback? If so, please fill in the information below:

Name _____

Church Name _____

Denomination _____ Church Size _____

Church Address _____

City _____ State _____ ZIP _____

Church Phone _____

E-mail _____